I Choose God

I CHOOSE GOD

Stories From Young Catholics

Edited by
Chris Cuddy and Peter Ericksen

PUBLISHED BY ST. ANTHONY MESSENGER PRESS
CINCINNATI, OHIO

Cover design by: LUCAS Art & Design, Grandville, Michigan
Cover image: Tina Chang / Getty Images
Book design by Phillips Robinette, O.F.M.

LIBRARY OF CONGRESS CATALOGING-IN-PUBLICATION DATA

I choose God : stories from young Catholics / edited by Chris Cuddy and Peter Ericksen.
   p. cm.
 Includes bibliographical references.
 ISBN 978-0-86716-773-3 (pbk. : alk. paper) 1. Catholic youth—Religious life. I. Cuddy, Chris. II. Ericksen, Peter.

BX2355.I35 2007
282.092'2—dc22
[B]
                           2007001777

ISBN 978-0-86716-773-3

Published by Servant Books, an imprint of
St. Anthony Messenger Press.
28 W. Liberty St.
Cincinnati, OH 45202
www.ServantBooks.org

Printed in the United States of America.
Printed on acid-free paper.

   08 09 10 11 5 4 3 2

Dedications

To Jim and Debbie Cuddy, who through their words and
actions first taught me what it means to be an adopted
son, loved by God and family.

–Chris Cuddy

To my grandparents:
To Clarice and Peter Edward, for always being there for
me in my spiritual journey, with your experienced
wisdom and warming hearts.

To Aunt Rosemary, who is like a grandparent, for your
tender care, thoughtfulness and enduring generosity.

To Margaret and Robert Matthias, for all your love and
prayers and enduring fidelity to Mother Church.
May this book bring you peace, solace and hope.
Yours is a Catholic faith I emulate.

–Peter Matthias Ericksen

Contents

Foreword

It's been over twenty years since I was received into the Catholic Church. And while some might argue that I'm now a *bona fide* "Catholic veteran," I have to be honest and say that in many ways I still feel more like "the new kid on the block." The life and heritage of the Church are so rich. Every time I go to Mass, pray the rosary or read a book by someone like Pope Benedict XVI, I'm overcome by how much our Lord still wants to give me.

One lifetime isn't enough to receive all the grace our Lord has prepared for us. That's why there's eternity.

I've been blessed with the opportunity to share my journey to Catholicism with people all around the world. And one of the most exciting things for me to see is how many young adults are discovering (or rediscovering) the fullness and beauty of the faith. I can't tell you how thrilled I am when I have the opportunity to sit down with young Catholics and hear how our Lord has brought them home to the Church.

I am delighted that there is finally a book written for Catholic young people *by* Catholic young people. The news media are saturated with stories about the violence, tragedy and anguish of that generation. However, our heavenly Father has promised never to forsake his people (see Hebrews 13:5). There is always a chosen remnant of his faithful. I firmly believe that this book will be a source of encouragement for those of us who are parents (or even grandparents), because it gives us a personal glimpse into the vibrant faith, hope and love of today's Catholic youth.

I also believe that this book will be a source of inspiration for other young people. While being young has never been easy, it's always been important. I love the words of Saint Paul to his friend Timothy: "Let no one despise your youth" (1 Timothy 4:12). We're all called to be God's children (see Matthew 18:3), and youth—whether it is physical or spiritual—is something to be cherished. It's never too early to enter into the eternal embrace of our heavenly Father. And his Church is never too full of people who wish to receive the fullness of his grace.

I strongly recommend this book to all who are interested in the spiritual journeys of today's youth and to all who seek inspiration for their own spiritual journey. May we be "eternally young" in the love of Jesus Christ, the eternal Son.

—Scott Hahn

Professor of Theology and Scripture
Franciscan University of Steubenville

Introduction

Give me chastity and continence, but not yet!"[1] This was the prayer of a young man who had one of the most amazing conversion stories of all time and certainly one of the most influential. He was handsome, young and driven by his passions. He was a man of the world—desiring money, power, girls and fame. And he was so talented that he often got what he desired.

His name was Augustine. Born into a religiously divided household, his Catholic mother tried to instill faith and virtue into her son, but Augustine rejected her beliefs about God. Living a life of unabashed hedonism and licentiousness, he stole, swindled and conceived a son out of wedlock. One can imagine how much pain he must have caused his mother, but she refused to lose hope and found solace in prayer.

Augustine had a near-death experience that caused him to take a serious look at the meaning and purpose of life. He had many questions, and he wasn't satisfied with the typical answers. He found himself yearning for something deeper, something more fulfilling, than the fleeting pleasures he'd been pursuing. The person and work of Jesus Christ attracted him.

Augustine's passions, however, still could erupt with seemingly uncontrollable power. While his spirit was becoming willing, his flesh remained weak. It took many years of struggle for him to make the firm and irrevocable decision to change his life.

Finally the partying was over. No longer would he give in to the illicit pleasures his body craved. No longer would he be a slave to lust. He would live for Christ and for Christ alone. Through the transforming grace of his heavenly Father, he found a new joy and happiness that went beyond his wildest expectations. In dying to himself he found true life, the eternal life of an adopted son of God.

Saint Augustine became one of the greatest bishops in the history of the Catholic Church and one of its most influential leaders and teachers. Recalling his struggles and conversion, he wrote the immortal words: "You have made us for yourself, and our heart is restless until it rests in you."[2]

Like Saint Augustine, many people today are searching for something more, something greater, something truly fulfilling. This book contains the accounts of young people, the authors included, who have found that something—truth, joy and fulfillment—in the Catholic Church. Some of us were raised Catholic, others were raised Protestant, and still others were raised without any religious formation at all. Yet the one thing that unites us is that the saving hand of Jesus Christ led us to a deep and bold love for his bride, the Catholic Church. We believe all that she teaches and professes. We confess her creed with our lips and strive to live out her morals in our lives.

These testimonies offer answers to many of the questions being hurled at today's young men and women—questions about life, death and eternity. Several of our contributors recount the "dark valleys" into which they meandered; some we identify by a pseudonymous first name because of the sensitive nature of their stories. Many contributors mention particular media that they found helpful in their search for the truth; we have included information about these and other materials in our "recommended resources" list at the back of the book.

For young Catholics who feel alone in their faith, let us assure you with the words of the great Pope John Paul II: "Be not afraid!" There are hundreds of thousands of young people just like you—young people who love Jesus and his Church. Don't give up when things grow difficult. Take life head-on and live for Christ.

And to parents and grandparents who have witnessed a loved one walking away from the Church, we also say, "Be not afraid." Though the tragedy is real, and your hearts may be burdened with worry, do not lose hope, and never stop praying. Many young people are returning to the splendor of Catholicism through the power of your love, example and prayer.

In his first address as pope, Benedict XVI stated:

I have before my eyes…the testimony of Pope John Paul II. He leaves a Church that is more courageous, freer, more youthful. She is a Church which, in accordance with his teaching and example, looks serenely at the past and is not afraid of the future.... I will continue our dialogue, dear young people, the future and hope of the Church and of humanity, listening to your expectations in the desire to help you encounter in ever greater depth the living Christ, eternally young.[3]

We offer this book as a gift to the Church and to our "eternally young" Savior—not to draw attention to ourselves but rather to be a testament to God's goodness and grace in our lives. For they are not just *our* stories; they are also *his* stories told through us.

—Chris Cuddy and Peter Ericksen

ONE

Madly in Love With Jesus

Father Donald Calloway

Being young is awesome! Yet do you still find yourself thirsty for meaning and purpose in life? What about real, hard-core, objective truth? Are you thirsty for that?

I bet you are. And guess what? I know where to find it, and I'll share it with you. *Be young and passionately Catholic!*

Huh?

Yeah, you read it right: *Be young and passionately Catholic.* You might be a little confused by this statement. How can "passionate" and "Catholic" go together?

Is there hope for us, living in a culture that constantly inundates us with consumerism, lust and religious pluralism? Definitely. There's always hope. Saint Paul said, "Where sin increased, grace abounded all the more" (Romans 5:20).

Trust me; I know. Before I fell madly in love with Jesus Christ and the Catholic Church, my life was full of youthful passions. I was heavily involved in drinking, drugs and pornography before I was a teenager. But wait, I'm just getting started.

My stepfather, an officer in the military, was stationed in Japan, so my family moved there when I was a teenager. I ran away from home at age fifteen, causing an international scene that led to my being kicked out of the country. Back in the United States, I dropped out of school and was forced to spend time in a drug rehabilitation center. At age eighteen I was thrown into jail during Mardi Gras, acquired a tattoo of the Grateful Dead and caught a venereal disease from somebody. I wore waist-length hair, funky clothes and earrings. I had a foul mouth and atheistic beliefs.

You get the picture: I was a pretty bad dude. I was lost and radically confused. Young? Yes. Happy and full of hope? Not even.

I exhausted the pleasures of the world in my hunger for fulfillment. I drank of every illicit pleasure the world extended to me, and I came up dry. The sweetness our culture offers left a bitter taste in my mouth and an emptiness in my soul. Little did I know the plan God had for my life.

My heart longed for something more. I desperately wanted to find a cause to believe in. I craved a purpose for my life that would transform my seemingly meaningless existence into true, everlasting happiness. I desired something that extends beyond this chaotic, temporal world. I desired something eternal.

At the age of twenty I hit rock bottom. I had nothing, and I was nothing. And that's when God revealed himself to me. When I had nothing to live for, he was my only hope.

He was the Father I had always had but never knew I needed.

It was a late night at our home in Norfolk, Virginia. In despair and boredom I picked up a book from my parents' shelf. It was about apparitions of the Blessed Virgin Mary. My parents had converted to Catholicism several years earlier, but I had remained unimpressed and unaffected by their newfound faith. This book caught my attention, however. I had never heard of such things before.

Forgetting all of my problems, fears and inner pain, I began reading. I finished the book by early morning, and my life was forever changed. No longer was I willing to be a slave of the flesh and passions of this world. From now on I would live under the lordship of Jesus Christ.

I was madly in love with Jesus, and I knew that I had to give my life completely to him. How could I turn away from such mercy and hope, from the reality that there actually is a God who loves me so radically that he suffered and died for me? Everything I had been searching for in life—purpose, happiness and peace—were to be found in knowing Jesus Christ. Only he could satisfy me.

As time went on, however, I was faced with a difficult situation: How was I supposed to know what Jesus wanted me to believe about serious moral issues like contraception, abortion, euthanasia and homosexuality? After all, many of these things aren't addressed explicitly in the Bible. To whom could I turn to find the answers to life's most challenging issues?

What I discovered was that in his infinite love, Jesus Christ doesn't want us to grope around in moral darkness. He doesn't expect us to stumble through life, formulating understandings of what is right and wrong based upon our own subjective convictions. Quite the contrary, actually: God has given us the Catholic Church—founded by Jesus Christ himself—and this is the way he continues to protect, guide and love his people. Our Savior promised us that no matter what oppositions, trials or difficulties arise, "the gates of Hades shall not prevail" against his Church (Matthew 16:18).

Catholicism gave me everything I had been craving: purpose in life, hope of eternal happiness and interior peace. No longer did I have to construct my "reality" upon the crumbling foundation of my own subjective interpretations and disordered desires. I had finally found true truth and real love. I had found the unsinkable ark of salvation.

I know it's not easy to be young and Catholic today. Our culture is saturated with many deadly distractions; many things seek to lure the heart and soul away from what is good, true and beautiful. I speak to young people all over the world, and I've heard their concerns, fears, worries, pains and anxieties. And I've been there myself.

In spite of all these things, however, I firmly believe that God is doing something truly wonderful in the hearts and lives of today's young people. They're tired of all the gray, subjective, rationalistic approaches to life. Like me, they've tried all that and found it lacking. Human wisdom will never satisfy the soul; only God can do that.

I am blessed to be a part of a generation of young Catholics who are in love with their faith. It is my sincere desire that others will join us in falling more deeply in love with our Lord, his mother and his Church.

TWO

Happy Hour

Brooke Burns

My conception of the ideal spring break during my junior year of college was quite simple: lazy days spent soaking in the hot desert sun while sipping on a cold beer and flirting with cute guys. Ironically, I really didn't have to wait for spring break in order to indulge in these activities; this was already how I spent most of my time.

I had no real cares apart from the never-ending drama surrounding which boy I liked and which gossiping girl I was mad at on any given day. Drinking was a daily activity for my friends and me, and it began the moment classes were over. Although most of us were underage, fake IDs facilitated our habit. I thought I was living life to its fullest, and I was making sure that I had a lot of fun along the way.

Life as I knew it came to a screeching halt when my mother informed our family that we were going on a pilgrimage to Medjugorje during *my* spring break. [Note: The Church has made no official statement regarding Medjugorje, but many people have had life-changing experiences there.] I was mortified. The thought of missing out on mindless activities with my friends—especially over an epic time like spring break—was devastating.

No matter how much I protested, resistance was futile: my mother had visited Medjugorje a few months earlier and had come back firmly resolved to take the rest of our family there later that year. The choice was out of my hands.

As the day of the trip drew closer, numerous thoughts and emotions ran through my mind and heart. I had no concrete idea about where I was going. *What am I getting myself into?* I asked myself over and over again. I had heard the claims that Mary was appearing to certain visionaries, but I didn't know the details. To be completely honest, Medjugorje scared me a little bit. It had the reputation for being "holy," and while I attended Mass on Sunday, I knew I was not nearly as sanctified as I should be.

Nothing could have prepared me for what I encountered in Medjugorje. In ten short days I witnessed an atheist's radical conversion to Christianity and had my first real—and honest—confession. Something beautiful and amazing happened: God's love touched my heart. As I was forced to let go of the world, I fell into the loving embrace of our Lord and Savior Jesus Christ, who had been waiting for me all along. I was convinced that I would live my life differently.

On Again, Off Again

The returning plane ride was extremely difficult. I had just experienced a taste of heaven on earth, and my heart longed to remain in that grace-filled place. Yet fear, anxiety and depression began to steal the peace of my soul as I contemplated what awaited me back home. I reminded myself that I was a changed young woman. I was confident that I could kick my old habits with the snap of my fingers.

Soon I was attending daily Mass, praying a daily rosary with my family and fasting on Wednesdays and Fridays. I even swore off drinking. Everything seemed to be going along perfectly. My faith was flourishing, and I still was able to maintain my relationships with my nonchurch friends. It was the best of both worlds—or so I thought.

Slowly but surely I became more lax in my walk with God. My prayer life began to wither. What began as one hour of daily prayer was eventually reduced to one Our Father. I began dating a young man who led our relationship down a path of pain and immorality. Soon I was going to the bars four nights a week and only attending classes every other day. I felt like a stranger to God.

My life had taken a complete 180-degree turn when I went to Medjugorje; now it was turning back. I had fooled myself into thinking it was possible to lead a "double life." Much to my chagrin, I had discovered that it was not possible to follow both Jesus and the world.

One Thursday evening I decided to attend Mass instead of making happy hour with the girls. My reason for choosing Mass over the bars was far from holy: I was low on money. God uses such circumstances.

A friend from high school approached me after Mass. She was beautiful and bubbly, and she always made it a point to invite me to hang out with her and her friends. However, as sweet as she was, she was definitely a "Jesus freak," and I figured her friends were even worse.

This friend asked if I was still living at home. I said that I was. She smiled, told me that I needed to grow up and insisted that I move in with her. My initial reaction was to make up some lame excuse. This was not the kind of person I envisioned myself living with. Yet deep inside I knew that I was standing at a crossroad in life. I knew that I wanted to follow God, and this could be an opportunity to begin the change I was craving.

After a couple days of contemplation, I decided to follow my gut instinct and accept her invitation. My new roommates welcomed me with open arms. It only took one day for me to feel completely comfortable around them. I could sense a sincere and genuine love in their presence that I had never felt with any of my other friends.

Within a week I met an amazing group of young people who were able to do what I had long thought was impossible: follow Jesus Christ *and* live life to its fullest. These people were thoroughly Catholic, and they knew how to have fun. There was never a dull moment with them.

Although I enjoyed my new friends, my old lifestyle kept beckoning, and I eventually slid back into my old ways. I hid everything from my roommates. In my heart I longed to tell them about my struggles, to let them know that I was living a double life, but I didn't think that they would understand where I was coming from because they were all such "goody-goodies."

I even became jealous about their courage to do what was right. *Why was it so easy for them yet so hard for me?* This jealousy turned into bitterness and anger, and I resolved even more not to share my struggles with them.

Free and Forgiven

One morning, around 5:30 AM, I awoke in my boyfriend's apartment and drove home. Hung over and tired, I couldn't wait to sleep in my own bed. I was a little nervous: My chances of running into my roommates were far greater at this time of day. I prepared an elaborate story to explain my absence if I was caught sneaking in.

As I stumbled up the steps, my roommate opened the front door. She firmly told me to sit down. "We need to talk." She explained that she had been up all night, worried, waiting for my return.

I was embarrassed. I felt as if I were fifteen years old again, and my mom had caught me sneaking in. The lump in my throat was so large that I couldn't swallow.

I made an earth-shattering realization that morning: My roommate was the first *real* friend that I had ever had. Without my saying anything she had sensed that something was wrong. She knew I had not been spending nights at my parents' house. She had noticed on more than one occasion that my breath reeked of alcohol.

I broke down—physically, emotionally and spiritually. My roommate didn't judge or condemn me. She listened to everything I had to say and seemed to understand my struggles. It was incredible. For the first time in my life I was free to explain my inner battle of living a life for the Lord and a life for the world.

That same day I broke up with my boyfriend and gave up my fake ID. I went to confession and allowed the Lord's mercy to envelop every inch of my body and soul. I firmly resolved to live each day fully for Jesus Christ. No longer could I live a life of dishonesty and lukewarmness.

I am not going to tell you that life has been all peachy ever since, for that is far from the case. The struggles and temptations remain. Every day I wake up and decide to give my life to the Lord, for without him I would fall right back into my old habits. It is through my "daily conversions" that I have found strength and healing.

The Lord sought me, forgave me and loved me. In my brokenness he gave me the inner strength to change my life and to begin living for him. And for this I am forever thankful.

THREE

The Fullness of Worship

Adam White

I'm often asked why I decided to convert to Catholicism. The short answer is that the grace of God led me to the realization that what I had thought was an antiquated, institutional body is actually the magnificent, eternally young sanctuary where the fullness of the Christian faith and God's truth are found.

Nevertheless, there isn't a day that goes by when I am not thankful for having been raised in a fervent evangelical home. Reading and memorizing Scripture, attending church and Sunday school, daily prayers: These were my habits from a very early age.

Truth be told, I suppose I've always been a Catholic. I was baptized in the Catholic Church as an infant, but shortly thereafter my parents, who were earnest Catholics, were invited to a Bible study with some Protestant friends. They found themselves (so they thought) unable to reconcile many of their Catholic beliefs with what they found in Scripture. So they left the Catholic Church, and we were henceforth Protestant Christians, saved from the "unnecessary" and "man-made" traditions of Roman Catholicism. We attended a church of the Pentecostal persuasion, but when that church virtually collapsed, we began attending the local Evangelical Free church.

Growing up I knew very little of Catholicism, except that much of my extended family was nominally Catholic. From all appearances theirs was hardly a life that could be called Christian. To me being a Christian meant being able to articulate something along the lines of "I have a personal relationship with Jesus." But for every Catholic I knew (a thundering total of fifteen or twenty), Mass attendance was occasional and perfunctory, and if asked about their faith they gave an indifferent response.

To be sure, a Catholic *could* be a Christian. But why anyone with a living, vibrant relationship with Christ would want to remain in the spiritual desert of Catholicism—when they could drink from the fresh waters of authentic biblical Christianity—was beyond me.

Lead Kindly, Liturgy

After graduating from high school, I studied at a small evangelical Christian college north of Boston. Having grown up simply following my parents to church every Sunday, I was more than a little bewildered and uncertain about where to worship. One week I would go to the local Baptist church, the next week a popular nondenominational church, to be followed by the Congregational church a week later. All of my friends went to different churches, and if someone had a late night on Saturday (I plead the

Fifth Amendment here), he or she didn't go to church at all. Simply staying home and reading the Bible would suffice.

During my junior year of college, one of my professors invited me to tag along to the Anglican church that he and his wife attended. I was rather dubious about the idea at first. A friend had told me that the Episcopal Church (the denominational name for the Anglican Church in America) was "kind of like a Catholic Church." The little I knew of liturgy seemed to suggest suffocation and constriction. Statues? Canned prayers? Bowing and crossing oneself? Yuck. The whole thing seemed sterile, dry and lifeless.

However, my first visit to the Church of the Advent in downtown Boston will be forever branded in my memory: the peal of the steeple bell echoing down the street as we ambled up to the church, the dimly lit nave with its gothic arches and the positively angelic choir. The majesty and resplendence of the liturgy transported me, and far from seeming rote and meaningless, the whole event seemed to animate and buoy my own efforts to worship the Most High. "My soul magnifies the Lord!" (Luke 1:46).

Where has this been my whole life? I wondered. Why had no one ever told me about liturgy? At this church people recited a second-century creed, flung incense and prayed the Angelus. They even sang in Greek and Latin—the Kyrie, the Sanctus, the Agnus Dei. These ancient rites did not inhibit or frustrate worship as I had suspected they would. Rather they seemed to free me from the shallow puddle of my own resources (to borrow a wonderful expression from author Thomas Howard).

Needless to say, I was dumbfounded. I felt as if my world had been turned upside down, for I had never expected to actually enjoy such worship. I had fallen head over heels in love with this ancient and glorious form of Christian worship known as liturgy.

Living the Truth

I began reading assiduously. I read Church history, the early Church Fathers and the writings of the saints. I read the stories of evangelicals who had actually converted to Roman Catholicism. In particular, I felt that Tom Howard's provocative little book *Evangelical Is Not Enough* had been written specifically for me. I was astonished that one man could articulate my own thoughts so precisely. I was completely engrossed by his account of his discovery of Anglicanism and eventual reception into the Catholic Church.

I subsequently made Dr. Howard's acquaintance, and he became a guide in my exploration of Catholicism. He patiently answered all of my questions and gave me books to read, as well as his friendship and love. One by one, all of my objections and suppositions about Catholicism began to evaporate, exposed as nothing more than misconceptions.

In my mind the burden of proof began to shift. The question changed from "Why should I ever become a Catholic?" to "Why should I remain separated from the ancient Church?" I realized that the unity of the Church—for which our Lord prayed in John 17:20–23—had meant more than a "spiritual unity" to the apostles. I learned that the Eucharist—the sacramental presence of Christ's Body, Blood, soul and divinity—had been the anchor of the Christian Church for centuries (see 1 Corinthians 11:23–26). Furthermore, Christ didn't leave us a Church that was dependent upon the personality and sermons of a particular pastor, however insightful he might be.

With alacrity and profound gratitude, I was formally received into the Catholic Church at the Easter Vigil in 2004. Some evangelical friends received the news of my conversion with derision and incredulity. Others congratulated me for pursuing what I thought was the best way for me to follow Jesus.

But that missed the point. Becoming a Catholic wasn't simply about an arbitrary preference for a certain style of worship, though I do love the liturgy. Rather it was about the truth. Specifically, I see the Catholic Church as the authoritative agent for safeguarding and proclaiming the Word of God, the sacraments and the unity befitting the body of Christ.

A famous cardinal once remarked that he loved the Church even though it was "mud-splashed from history." It is true: The Catholic Church has had its share of corruption and scandal. Consisting of sinful, weak human beings (like myself), it is continually in need of renewal. However, I am confident that our Lord will keep the promise he made to Peter about his Church: It will withstand all of the fury and vehemence that hell wages against it (see Matthew 16:18).

The Church, described by Saint Paul as the "pillar and bulwark of the truth" (1 Timothy 3:15), is in its essence the pure and spotless bride of Christ, despite the manifold shortcomings and failures of its members. I thank God that I am now a member of this one, holy, Catholic and apostolic Church—to whose bountiful table I come hungry and needy.

FOUR

Accepted by Christ

Melanie Welsch

I attended a forty-thousand-student college that *Playboy* magazine voted a top ten party school. Supermodel-type girls and athletic frat boys surrounded me. Sex, drugs and booze were available to any person at any time. In my coed dorm the guy next door grew pot in his room and was responsible for the face and body piercings of half the freshmen on our floor. The guy at the end of the hall contracted an incurable sexually transmitted disease during the first week of school.

In spite of all this chaos, I was certain that I was strong enough to handle the temptations.

The summer before my sophomore year of high school, my mother had forced me to go on a Life Teen trip. I was certain that I was going to hate every minute of it. In addition, I was certain that I was not going to become friends with a bunch of "Jesus freaks."

I was wrong. Not only did I make friends, but I also became a "Jesus freak." At a Mass with six hundred other young Catholics on the beach, I felt the presence of God for the first time.

I returned to my high school a changed person. I began sporting a new wardrobe of shirts imprinted with things like "Proud to be Catholic," and I wore a large wooden cross around my neck. With my new knowledge of God and Catholicism, I became an instant evangelist sharing my faith and excitement with every person I knew.

My friends had a little trouble grasping this "new me." Surprisingly, however, they never abandoned me. People started calling me "Mother Teresa," but I didn't mind. I loved Mother Teresa, and their jokes inspired me to follow Jesus all the more.

Ironically, the people who made fun of me also nominated me for homecoming queen and winter courts queen. I had the best of both worlds. I could proclaim my faith and still feel accepted by my peers.

My Big Secret

Something changed the summer before I went to college. The thought of going off to a new place and having to make new friends made me nervous. I already had friends in high school before I rediscovered the Catholic faith. Things would be different in college. No one would know me, and I was worried that I would be deemed a "Jesus freak" and rejected.

Fearing that people wouldn't give me a chance if they knew about my faith, I came up with a brilliant idea: I decided not to tell anyone that I was Catholic—at least, not right away. I decided just to be a "good person," and eventually—after I had made a lot of friends—I would reveal my true self.

I moved into the dorms determined to be popular, and it happened pretty fast. I was able to fit into any group. I was like a chameleon. I didn't hesitate to talk, dress or even dance in ways that fit with my peers. I would hang out with my new "friends" while they drank or did drugs. I knew what they were doing was wrong, and I never took part in their behavior, but I also didn't express my disapproval. I wanted to be accepted by the group.

I successfully flew under the radar. My friends assumed that I was just like them. And all along I still considered myself to be the good Catholic girl I had been before. It took one of them to show me what I had become.

Nick was the muscular, tan, dark-haired guy who lived across the hall. He was the kind of guy whom every girl liked and every guy wanted to be. He paid a lot of attention to me. We spent time together and got to know each other pretty well—or so I thought.

One day Nick commented on my outfit as I walked down the hall. "You look really good. Where are you going?"

We were well into the college semester. I was confident in my friendships, and I decided that it was time to come clean about being Catholic. In fact, I thought Nick might be impressed to discover that I was a Christian girl with values.

"I'm going to church," I responded, batting my eyes.

He didn't hide his surprise. "*You're* going to church?"

"Yeah, I go to church every Sunday." I went on to tell

him about how I was this *really* Catholic girl and that my nickname used to be "Mother Teresa." I thought this new information was impressing him until he spoke again in that same confused voice: "Huh! I would have never guessed that *you* were Catholic."

I was stunned. "Why not?"

He chuckled and said, "I just never would have guessed it by the way you dress, the way you talk, the jokes you tell and the way you dance. Wow! I just never would have guessed that!"

I was crushed. Nick served me the biggest piece of humble pie I'd ever had. My stomach was in my throat, and tears welled up in my eyes. It took all the control I could muster not to break down in front of him. It felt as if a knife was piercing my heart.

A New Awakening

When I came back from Mass, I went into my room, curled up in a little ball and cried. I don't mean just a few tears; I mean ugly sobbing, loud crying. Had you seen me, you would have thought someone had died. And someone had. That pious Catholic girl I thought myself to be was gone.

I got up from my bed, turned on the light and looked at my reflection in the mirror. I didn't recognize myself. I didn't know who I was or what I stood for. I was leading a double life. I was broken.

In desperation I called the girl who had mentored me in the faith during high school. Crying, I told her everything.

"Melanie," she said, "when you entered college your goal was to fit in, make friends and have fun. You did all that, but how's that working for you? Does it make you happy?"

Honestly, there had been times when I had a lot of fun. But, no, I wasn't content, I wasn't joyful, and I wasn't truly happy. In fact, even though I was surrounded by a plethora of "friends," never had I felt so alone and empty in all my life.

My mentor then asked me, "When was the last time you felt truly happy? When were the times in your life when you felt full of joy?"

Surprisingly, I didn't even have to think about it. "It was when we had Mass on the beach, and that time we went to World Youth Day and saw Pope John Paul II, and that time we went on that Mexico mission trip and helped all those poor people."

I went on and on until my friend stopped me and pointed out that all of the things I had listed were related to God and his transforming grace. This was where I had found happiness before. This was the only place where I could find true happiness again.

In high school I had made a lot of little decisions that strengthened my faith. I chose to do things that would lead me closer to God. I had made decisions that were good and true to the person I was inside. In college, however, I had made a lot of little decisions that broke my relationship with the Lord. I had sold out. I wasn't living the faith; I was just going through the motions.

I had failed because I thought the only requirements for being a "good Catholic" were attending Mass on Sunday and remaining a virgin. Now I realized that that wasn't enough. I wanted joy again; I longed for peace.

Jesus once said, "I came that they may have life, and have it abundantly" (John 10:10). I knew that it was the Lord who was going to bring me joy; it was Jesus Christ who was going to fill me up again. I went to confession the next day, and the power of God's love and mercy overwhelmed me.

Change happened within me when I began making good decisions in every area of my life: dress, speech, dance and entertainment. Only when I was completely aligned with God's will did I discover my true identity. Only then did he reveal to me my deep worth and dignity.

FIVE

Saying Yes to the Light

Therese

I grew up in a family that did not practice any religion. When I was young we lived in a small town in southern California where there was a lot of violence. Our house was broken into a few times, and we had several bikes stolen. I remember running to and from friends' houses, afraid that something might happen to me. From an early age I thought that this world was a dark and scary place.

My family moved to Colorado when I was eleven. Life continued to be hard but in different ways. In middle school some of the boys who rode my bus constantly ridiculed, hit and pushed me. I remember frequently getting off the bus, running to my room and crying for hours.

I grew to dislike myself and became very unsure of who I was. I felt that my identity was being taken away from me, and I grew very quiet and reserved.

Confronting the Darkness

Because of my negative experiences in middle school, I was afraid to start high school. Moreover, I thought that if boys were going to like me, I would have to change my appearance. I became obsessed with my weight, worked out all the time and ate next to nothing.

On April 20, 1999, my life changed forever. I was a sophomore at Columbine High School in Littleton, Colorado. As I was sitting in a class right before lunch, the feeling that I should leave school overwhelmed me. My habit at the time was to meet my friend Rebekah in the library, where we would study during our lunch period. That day, however, I told Rebekah that there was no way I was going to remain at school for lunch.

Rebekah wanted to stay and study for an upcoming test, but I was resolved to leave. I suggested that we go to a restaurant and study there. She objected that she didn't have any money, and I told her that I would pay. She eventually agreed, and we set off for a bagel shop. I was not supposed to have a car for another year, but for some reason my parents had changed their minds the week before.

As we were driving away, I looked into my rearview mirror and noticed hundreds of students running out of the school. We soon discovered that there had been a shooting: Twelve students and one teacher had been killed before the two gunmen committed suicide. It was only later that I found out that most of the shootings had happened in the library, and that the two gunmen must have been walking into the school as we were walking out!

I wondered what—or *who*—had given me that overwhelming urge to leave school and why my life had been spared. When I shared my story with people after the shooting, they usually told me that God was watching over me, that he didn't want me to die and that he had a great plan for my life.

I began to pray every day. More than anything else I prayed for God's protection. At the same time, I could not understand what kind of God would allow something so tragic to happen.

The following year, wanting to be accepted by others and not really understanding what had happened at my school, I fell into drinking and partying. I continued to worry about my weight, and this anxiety consumed most of my thoughts.

I couldn't stand the emptiness I felt, and I eventually distanced myself from the party crowds and fell into a deep depression. Finally, at the end of my junior year, one of my classmates committed suicide, and the thought occurred to me: *If he was in so much pain and he took his life, and I am in so much pain, then the way out of all this is for me to take my life as well.*

The depression hit the hardest during my senior year. I would sit in my room, think about life and remember all of the hurtful things that had been said about me. Staring into a mirror, I would cut myself while tears rolled down my face. I would often cry myself to sleep.

The world continued to darken. I was so confused. I felt as if I had nothing to live for. I wanted to die, but I was afraid of death.

Discovering God

Just when things were becoming tremendously difficult—when I began to think that there was no way I could continue in this world—one of my friends invited me to a Catholic Church. A youth minister greeted me as soon as I walked through the door. I immediately sensed something different about her—something different *within* her: She was bright and full of life. I knew she had something that I didn't have.

The youth minister began inviting me out for coffee. She told me about a God who was passionately in love with me. I didn't think anyone could love me, but I could feel God's love radiating from her. My face lit up and my heart leapt as she spoke the words I longed to hear: "God loves you."

Eventually, after going on a youth retreat and meeting other people who had the same light I sensed in that youth minister, I decided to become Catholic. I finally saw that God was the only one who could fill my emptiness. He was the one I had been missing all my life.

The following summer I told another youth minister that I no longer wanted to end my life and that I wanted to give myself entirely to Christ. He advised me to go to the Franciscan University of Steubenville, where I could be immersed in the Catholic faith and in Catholic life.

My parents told me that there was no way they could afford the tuition. Then one day it seemed as though God had changed their hearts: They told me that I could go and that they would help me in any way they could.

I enrolled at Franciscan University, and on March 30, 2002, I was received into the Catholic Church. Never before had I experienced as much joy and peace as I did the night that I came into the Church.

Even as a new Catholic, the next few years were very hard. I still needed a lot of healing in my life. God continued to care for me, and I learned to rely on him more and more. He continued to bring people into my life who guided me closer to him. I continued to seek counseling and meet with a spiritual director. Most importantly, I continued to pray. To this day God pours his joy, healing and wisdom into my life.

I have spent a lot of time reflecting on the events of my life—especially the events surrounding the Columbine shooting. Although I know that God did not delight in the death of those people, I also know that he was able to use this tragedy to draw people like me closer to him.

Two of the students who were killed during the shooting are thought to have responded *yes* when the gunmen asked if they believed in God. I think I would have said whatever I thought the gunmen wanted to hear. I had no idea who God was, and I questioned whether he even existed. Now I pray that I would say *yes* without hesitation.

Through their *yes* those two girls gave themselves to Christ even as their lives were being taken from them. With my life I am able to say *yes* by living for Christ and giving myself to him each and every day. I am so thankful that

God has called me to himself and that he has brought me to this beautiful place in life.

There was a time when I wouldn't have believed that this love and happiness were even possible. Now I can't wait to see what God has in store for me in the future. "God is light and in him is no darkness at all" (1 John 1:5).

SIX

Finding True Love

Josh Schwartz

I am the eldest of two children. My father was a self-proclaimed Conservative Jew. My mother was a typical American Catholic—faithful to the teachings she understood but poorly instructed in important areas of the faith.

I was your average "cradle Catholic." Baptized as an infant, I went to church weekly, received all the relevant sacraments and, sadly, did little more to pursue God. I believed in God during those early years, but I couldn't explain the basic tenets of the Catholic faith. I could recite the Golden Rule, the "law of love" and a few of the Ten Commandments. This, however, was the extent of my Catholic understanding, and it remained such through my adolescent years all the way to college.

As I grew older, being "religious" wasn't cool, and I began looking for excuses to write off the whole "church thing." I much preferred staying at home and watching football to going to church. During college my indifference toward Christianity turned into contempt.

One of my philosophy classes ignited my disdain. I found the readings fascinating, and for the first time in my life I became excited about learning. Our professor discussed all the hot topics of the day: abortion, euthanasia and homosexuality. He attacked religion in general—and Christianity in particular—as being narrow-minded and judgmental.

By the end of that semester, I had written off my faith. I became an ardent opponent of organized religion. The mere mention of anything Catholic or even Christian made me bristle with antagonism.

I enjoyed heated debates with family and friends about various issues related to religion and morality. I considered people of faith to be simple-minded. It seemed to me that they were weak and needed someone else to tell them what was right and wrong.

Faithful Friends

In the midst of this spiritual crisis, I met Amanda. She was a Baptist, though not a practicing one. Because a relationship can be truly successful only when God is at the center, ours was destined for failure right from the start. I did not understand the concept of complete, self-giving love. To me a significant other was merely a means to an end: my means to feeling good about myself.

One day, however, Lee, a friend on the University of Texas football team, asked me to join him and a few teammates at a Champions for Christ Bible study. Although I wasn't interested in learning about the Bible, my borderline obsession with athletics led me to go anyway.

The passion these individuals had for life, Jesus and the Scriptures amazed and enticed me. People were quoting Bible verses, giving testimonies, dancing and singing.

A girl asked me, "Are you hot or cold?" Dumbfounded, I asked her to repeat the question. She did and added a warning that being lukewarm was the worst of all answers. She read from Scripture: "So, because you are lukewarm, neither cold nor hot, I will spew you out of my mouth" (Revelation 3:16).

Wanting to fit in, I assured the girl that I was "hot" for Jesus, although this would not become a reality for several more months.

I began studying the Bible on my own. Amanda and I started discussing God and religion. I attempted to pull back from sin. I even began to join Amanda at her Baptist church services. However, I still wasn't ready to commit to organized religion.

Somewhere along the way, the topic of our future as a couple came up. Strangely, I made the comment that "my wife and kids *will* be Catholic" when we were discussing marriage and children. It is weird that I said this, because I wasn't even sure whether *I* would return to the Catholic Church.

Amanda was open to the idea. I was unaware that she had been reading about the Church on her own. In fact, she probably knew more about the Church than I did.

Then one day Amanda asked me, "Why do Catholics put so much emphasis on Mary?"

"What?" I replied.

She repeated her question. I was stuck! I had no idea.

Amanda then revealed that she had been reading *Catholicism for Dummies*. While she had found some things interesting, there were other things that really bothered her. She found the "Catholic obsession" with Mary to be particularly disturbing, and because of this she had decided that she would never convert.

In order to regain control of the situation, I began arguing with her. Granted, I didn't know what I was talking about, but I attempted to manipulate her all the same.

My ignorance of Scripture led me to misuse the one verse I knew: Ephesians 5:22–24:

> Wives, be subject to your husbands, as to the Lord. For the husband is the head of the wife as Christ is the head of the Church, his body, and is himself its Savior. As the Church is subject to Christ, so let wives also be subject in everything to their husbands.

I told Amanda that for her to be my wife, she would have to submit to my spiritual leadership. Sadly, I completely missed the beauty of Christ's self-sacrifice for his bride, the Church.

Amanda replied, "Well, I will submit to my husband, but I am not going to submit to an incompetent leader, and you don't even go to church!" The truth in her response was cutting. I can feel the dagger in my heart to this day. I realized the absolute hypocrisy in which I was living.

Faith and Forgiveness

Amanda and I grew apart over the next few weeks, and my attempts to fill my spiritual void failed. Feeling depressed and desperate, I called my mother and sister for advice. They told me to go to confession and Mass, but I wasn't interested.

"I have never *felt* God," I told them. "I've tried the 'God thing,' and it doesn't work for me."

"Well, everyone goes through that sometimes," my mom replied.

Frustrated, I responded, "You're not listening. I said *never!* I don't believe in the whole 'faith thing.'"

In spite of this I remained somewhat open to what my mom and sister were saying. After all, nothing else seemed to be working. *Maybe I should give Mass and confession a chance after all.*

In desperation I went to see a priest at a local Catholic church. He was a true spiritual father. He heard my confession, and I immediately felt as if a tremendous weight had been lifted from my shoulders. I felt free.

I decided to attend Mass that same day. Providentially, the Gospel reading was John 20:24–30, Jesus' encounter with the disciples—particularly Thomas—after the Resurrection. The priest gave a homily based on the verse "Blessed are those who have not seen and yet believe" (John 20:29). His words pierced my heart. Tears poured from my eyes as I felt my loving Father in heaven embrace me, his long-lost son. At that moment I knew my life would never be the same.

I still had some serious concerns about various theological, philosophical and moral issues. I wouldn't be completely satisfied until my newfound desire to follow God was united with a properly formed intellect. In order to find answers to my questions, I began to read. I devoured *Surprised by Truth*, *Rome Sweet Home*, *Catholicism and Fundamentalism* and countless other books on the Catholic faith. The answers in these books reassured me that the Catholic Church was truly where I needed to be.

As my understanding grew, so did my passion for the faith. The more I read, the more I wanted to share the treasures I had discovered in the Catholic Church. And the more I shared with people, the more I realized I needed to continue learning.

This intense process lasted for about a year. I became devoted to God and to God alone. Women were out of the picture. I needed time to heal and grow. Little did I know that God was preparing me for something more: He was preparing me to meet my future wife.

Katie was the daughter of a Baptist minister. She had an obvious love for God and was a committed seeker of truth. Prayerfully learning from my past mistakes, I applied all of the lessons about truth and love in my relationship with her. And I was never more convinced of these truths than when I witnessed Katie's own conversion to Catholicism. At that moment I realized that everything else in my life had been preparing me to live out my vocation as a husband, father and ultimately a son of God.

SEVEN

Never Letting Go

Liz Brown

It is easier for me to remain silent than to recount the story of my abortion experience and my eventual liberation from the culture of death. Mine is a difficult story of struggling with the shame involved in such a "choice" and the fear of what some may think. It is my hope that by sharing my journey from rebellion to repentance, anguish to absolution and death to the knowledge of life-giving love, others will be released from the lie of "abortion without consequences." It is only when we are released from the scourge of this lie that true healing can begin.

Fifteen years ago I was a terribly broken woman without a foundation. I had no true joy. I was lost. I hardly valued my own life, much less the life of another, and darkness surrounded me. All of this because I had taken the life of my child.

Many "seeds" had germinated into this catastrophic decision. My upbringing had been rocky soil for holiness but fertile ground for the culture of death. I experienced the tragic loss of my mother at an early age, and I was subjected to abuse. I had no consistent religious training.

These facts are no excuse for the choice I made. Many people experience these life events without sinning in such a grievous way. I made sinful choices that resulted in a deep separation between Jesus Christ and me. This disorder in me and in my relationships culminated in the ultimate disorder of abortion.

At the time I felt perfectly justified in my decision. Most of the people around me didn't have a problem with abortion. My politics supported my position and furthered my belief that this was *my* body and that I had the right— even the responsibility—to choose abortion. *You're not married. It's just tissue. You aren't financially secure. Your life will change forever with a baby. Mom and Dad mustn't find out. You won't be able to finish your degree. It won't be a big deal if you get the abortion early enough.* These are the words I told myself.

But honestly, I probably would have used *any* excuse to become free of the reality of being pregnant. There was no real love inside of me. I was empty. I had nothing within me that could offer the gift of life through adoption or attract the assistance of friends.

Neither had I the ability or desire to reach out to a Savior. After all, from my perspective I had no sin to be saved from. I was cut off from my womanhood, and I hated God. I willingly exchanged the truth for a life of lies.

From Death to Life

Little did I know how my abortion would change my life. Confusion, persistent thoughts of hell, depression and suicidal impulses descended upon me. *Why am I suddenly and intensely experiencing these things?* Abortion was supposed to be the "perfect solution"; after all, "it" wasn't a child. What was going on?

I spent thousands of dollars on counseling and medications, all in a desperate attempt to find love and wholeness. No one ever addressed the deep scars caused by the abortion. I didn't face the wounds I suffered in denying my nature as nurturer and protector of life. I remained very alone and very empty.

Amid this destruction Jesus was still at work. And even though I couldn't see it, he was showing me mercy through my pain. He was drawing me close, closing off escape routes and tearing down gradually the wall of my denial. His still, small, gentle voice kept asking me difficult questions: "Why are you afraid of hell when you don't believe in me? Why do you feel anxiety every time you see a pro-life bumper sticker? Why does every relationship you enter into seem to go nowhere? What is that deep sadness inside of you that has no name?"

I lived with these torments for three years, desperately trying to force them into the recesses of my mind. They emerged with particular clarity when I first met my husband, Peter, who was in the process of rediscovering his Catholic faith. When I told him of my abortion experience, his words pierced my heart: "Liz, abortion is wrong. You have sinned against God."

No one ever had talked to me this way. Peter didn't back down when I discussed the usual litany of excuses and mitigating circumstances. All the emotions I had tried to suppress erupted. I was at a crossroad, and I knew it. I could continue to walk to the death of my soul, or I could repent and walk toward life. I decided to choose life.

God meets us where we are, but he loves us too much to let us stay there. One year later, as I began my healing journey to Jesus Christ and his Catholic Church, the crooked path on which I had been walking began to be straightened. Through the sacraments I was immersed in the deep ocean of God's mercy and the fire of his consuming love.

As I confessed my sin of abortion, I mustered up the courage to look at the priest. He was crying—not only for the injustice done to my child but for my pain as well. Through this servant of God, I saw Jesus' face and received his eternal forgiveness.

In the Eucharist I found what I had been searching for: life in abundance. More than a sign of his faithfulness, Christ was offering me real and lasting participation in his heavenly banquet.

Healing Within

Recovering from abortion and its wounds takes time; it is a process. The tentacles of evil reach deep and have enduring consequences. I experienced this reality in my struggles with infertility and miscarriage.

I also was diagnosed with a rare form of ovarian cancer. The pain of the cancer was nothing compared to the despair I felt in my soul at the prospect of never bearing children. I was overcome with grief as I thought about the relationship between my "choice" so very long ago and my present agony.

I availed myself of the Catholic Church's post-abortion healing resources. I needed to take full responsibility for my past actions. I needed to understand the impact of my sinful choices without falling into despair. I needed to learn what it means to be a woman of God, what a healthy male-female relationship should look like and what a precious gift our Savior has given us in our sexuality.

This work of healing was very difficult at times, but it was well worth the effort. I received God's love and mercy, and he reminded me time and time again that his love is powerful enough to overcome the sins of all people, even those who have taken the life of an innocent little baby.

Through this healing process I have experienced moments of profound sweetness and joy that would have been impossible before my healing. In my journey something good and pleasing has flowered, not from my abortion experience (because abortion is *always* wrong) but in spite of my abortion.

My daughter's name is Rebecca, and my son by miscarriage is Michael. Rebecca has forgiven me for what I did to her—of this I am sure—and one day, God willing, I will behold her beautiful face in heaven, as well as that of Michael. For now, however, I must wait, and this saddens my heart more than you can know. Every fiber of my being longs to be a mother to my babies here on earth. But I have come to know the true meaning of love by bearing this cross, and I am growing in love for my God, my children and myself.

Job 12:10 reminds us that "in his hand is the life of every living thing and the breath of all mankind." It is there—in his loving grasp—that my daughter and son rest. I did nothing to deserve the gift of my heavenly relationship with my Maker and my two babies, but I have received it nonetheless.

This is my love letter to my daughter, Rebecca. In some small, humble way, I hope it honors her existence—her life. For she *is* real, she is a part of me, and I will never let her go again!

EIGHT

College Conversion

Chris Cuddy

I hated the Catholic Church, hated it with a passion. I devoured books, magazines and tapes that proclaimed the evils of Rome. I thought that anyone who occupied the papal office was the anti-Christ. I abhorred icons and statues of Mary and the saints. I detested the rosary. I considered the Mass to be idolatrous. In short, I was quite convinced that the Catholic Church was "the whore of Babylon" described in Revelation 14.

All of this before I was eighteen years old.

I was a first-semester college freshman enrolled at one of the most prestigious evangelical Protestant colleges in the country. I was double majoring in theology and philosophy, and my life's dream was to become a Protestant seminary professor. My grandfather was an evangelical pastor, and my uncle was a Presbyterian elder.

My childhood heroes included Martin Luther and John Calvin. I was deeply committed to the Protestant notions of justification by faith alone and the Bible as the sole source of Christian authority. I believed that Reformed theology (also known as Calvinism) was just a nickname for biblical Christianity. I was a staunch adherent to the famous "five points of Calvinism," which stress man's total depravity in relation to God's utter sovereignty. My sole desire was to delve ever deeper into Reformed thought and to help others deepen their Calvinistic affirmations and convictions.

Little did I know that things were about to change.

My Tour Guide

Most pilgrimages are not traveled alone, nor are they self-commissioned. There is usually someone who has made the trip before and is acquainted with the challenges that lie before the pilgrims. My guide on my pilgrimage to the Catholic Church was Scott Hahn.

Dr. Hahn's story had always been a puzzle to me. I had read his book *Rome Sweet Home* and had listened to the tape of his conversion story while I was in junior high. He was someone from my own theological "mold," so to speak: a committed Calvinist and Presbyterian, very anti-Catholic and very passionate about the Lord and his written Word. And yet he defected to Rome. How could this be?

My conclusion was that Scott Hahn was either a "flake" or a "fake." Either he was too blind and ignorant of the full majesty and richness of the Reformed tradition, or he was out to make a name for himself and willing to sell his soul to the devil in the process.

Through a series of providential events, I became acquainted with Scott shortly after I settled in at college. He was visiting my campus one evening in late September, and after a brief introduction, he invited me out to dinner so that we could "talk theology." I admit that I was a bit intimidated at the prospect of talking theology with a *Catholic* theologian, but I agreed. It couldn't hurt anything, right?

Dr. Hahn and I immediately clicked in a real and vibrant "brothers in Christ" kind of way. Through the majority of our initial three-and-a-half-hour conversation, neither of us brought up any distinctively Catholic beliefs. We spent most of our time talking about theological topics of mutual interest and swapping stories of theological heroes we both shared. I was shocked by how easy the conversation was and how much unity we had in our doctrines and beliefs.

I discovered that Dr. Hahn did not despise his former Protestant professors and colleagues. On the contrary, he explained that while he had changed his mind on certain issues, his respect for his Protestant mentors had increased over the years. This surprised me, but I believed him. He had a real sincerity and zeal for God and his truth.

We eventually came around to discussing some of our Catholic-Protestant disagreements. However, because it was late, we didn't get to examine the issues in a thorough fashion. Thus Dr. Hahn recommended several book titles and gave me his contact information in case I wanted to dialogue further.

I still remember shaking his hand and saying good-bye after dinner. My mind kept replaying our conversation as I walked back to my dorm.

Faith Crisis

To be honest, I really didn't expect the books that Scott Hahn recommended to be very persuasive. I flipped through several of the titles, and I shelved most of them, thinking that I might get around to reading them when I had some extra time on my hands. One of the book titles did catch my eye, however: *Catholic for a Reason*. I looked at the subtitle: *Scripture and the Mystery of the Family of God*. My curiosity piqued, I opened the book and decided to read the introduction "just to get a feel" for what the book was arguing. I thought I would read it for no more than ten minutes.

My "feel" quickly turned into a full-fledged intellectual immersion. I couldn't put the book down. In fact, I read the entire book twice in one sitting, and then I began poring through the other titles Dr. Hahn had recommended. One book turned into two. Two turned into four. By the end of that month, I had worked my way through about forty books on numerous issues in Catholic theology, apologetics and history.

Never before had I come across such clear, intelligible, scripturally saturated explanations of Catholic teaching. I quickly learned that my previous understanding of Catholicism was extremely misinformed. Soon I was completely enamored with the Catholic vision of God and reality.

It was late October when all of this came to a head. I was in a true crisis of faith. The only thing that I could do to keep my sanity was to keep studying, with the prayerful hope that everything would work out in the end. Thus I threw all formal academic caution to the wind. I began skipping classes on a regular basis and even missing meals. My grades and my appearance began to suffer, but I didn't care. I needed the security of knowing where I stood in relation to the Catholic Church. This was absolutely essential to my personal peace and sense of well-being.

During this time Dr. Hahn and I had several lengthy telephone conversations about the things I was reading. He wasn't pushy. He merely answered my questions, and he encouraged me to keep reading and praying. The more I read, the more I prayed. And the more I prayed, the more I felt that maybe, just maybe, the Catholic Church might be calling me home. It was time to make a decision.

God's Timing

I remember the day very vividly. It was a slow afternoon. I was sitting in my dorm room praying. I had just finished a chapter from a book by a Catholic theologian on the Church's teaching about salvation. Never before had I heard the saving gospel of Jesus Christ described as divine sonship. I had always thought that justification was mere legal acquittal. This theologian was telling me that it was much more than that: It is divine adoption. Salvation means being made a son of God.

With tears in my eyes, I bowed my head and gave consent. While I knew that I still had much to learn, the books that I had read were enough to persuade me that the

Catholic Church really was the Church Christ had instituted. All doubts were gone. It was time to come home.

I looked up, and my eyes were drawn immediately to the calendar hanging on the wall next to my desk. I looked at the date: it was October 31, 2002. I couldn't help but smile at God's ironic timing. Previously October 31 had been a very special day to me, for it was on October 31, 1517, that a young Martin Luther nailed his revolutionary Ninety-five Theses to the church door of Wittenberg, Germany, lighting the spark that ignited the flames of the Protestant Reformation.

On the anniversary of the beginning of the Protestant Reformation, I became Catholic. While I had yet to go through the RCIA program—I was officially received into the Catholic Church the following Easter Vigil—my heart had given consent to Catholicism. My pilgrimage was over. I was home.

NINE

Living in Christ

Julie Ericksen

Few memories are as vivid as that of the day I almost died.

It was a bright, sunny weekend during my first month of college, and my family had come to visit. We were scheduled to meet at my roommate's parents' house, which was close to campus. Four friends and I piled into a car and set off. Our destination was only two miles away.

We were driving toward the western sky with the bright sun in our eyes, when suddenly our laughing and talking turned to screaming. Unaware of a freight train traveling at full speed, we had driven directly in front of it. The back end of our car was struck, and we flew, spinning in the air, to the other side of the tracks.

As soon as we had been hit, a voice spoke to me. It told me that something bad had happened, but I would be fine. The voice was strong, and I felt it deep within my soul.

After the car came to a standstill, I looked into the back seat where my three friends had been sitting only moments before. The seat looked empty, and the back window was blown out. I panicked and struggled to open my door. It was jammed. My roommate was able to get out on her side, and I followed her out.

I had difficulty walking. There was a sharp pain and stiffness in my neck, and my legs were weak. We scanned the area, desperately looking for our missing friends. Our eyes eventually rested upon two of them lying in the middle of the road. Neither of them appeared to be moving. My roommate ran to one girl, and I ran to the other. I was unable to cry, and breathing became difficult.

I looked around but didn't see my other friend. I ran back to the crumpled wreck and anxiously peered through the hole where the window had been. I saw my friend lying motionless across the seat.

I slowly stepped away from the car, and I began to weep uncontrollably. It was so difficult for me to comprehend what had happened. I heard sirens in the distance, and a crowd of observers began to form.

My roommate's brother, who lived close by, was one of the first to arrive at the scene. He called my family, and it seemed like only seconds later that I saw my sister running toward me and my mother weeping in the distance. Not yet knowing exactly what had happened, we fell into each other's panicked embrace.

I was rushed to a nearby hospital for treatment of some minor injuries. In a stupor I walked into the hospital waiting room where my friends' parents were grieving over the loss of their daughters. Never before had I seen people so devastated. They hugged me, and we cried together. I tried to express to them how sorry I was for their loss.

One of the mothers took me in her arms and with a trembling voice said, "Live on for my daughter." I told her that I would, and we continued to weep together.

I wondered, *Why me? Why were my friends' lives taken and my life preserved?* I now had a responsibility to live a good life. But I wondered, *What is a good life?*

Looking for Answers

My life before the accident had been great. I had a loving family, a good education and a list of exciting opportunities before me. Now, for the first time in my life, I was forced to spend time thinking about the meaning of pain and suffering. I was overwhelmed with feelings of apprehension, wonder, unworthiness and shame. I didn't know what to do. I was confused.

I was born Catholic. I had been baptized and had even received my First Communion. When I was ten years old, my family decided to leave the Catholic Church and become Lutheran. There was no real *substance* to my faith. I knew that I should love God, love my neighbor and live a good Christian life, but that was it.

My life was too complex at this point; I needed more. I needed to know *how* to love God and *how* God loves us. I needed to know why God had permitted my friends to die such a horrible death.

After a week of recovery at home, I went back to college and tried to finish out the semester as best I could. With the help of counseling and talking to good friends, I was able to deal with the experience, but I wasn't completely satisfied. I needed to find answers to the painful questions that haunted me every day: *Why did this happen? Why did I survive?*

Unfortunately, I searched for answers in all the wrong places. I was extremely insecure about the purpose, meaning and future of my life, and I sought acceptance wherever I could. I became involved with the college party scene. At first I felt uncomfortable, but I quickly became desensitized. I engaged in behavior that I once had considered sinful. I drank heavily, partying on weekdays as well as weekends.

After a year of nonstop partying, I became friends with a boy named Peter. He and I would debate heatedly, often late into the night, about how damaging my partying was. I argued that my party friends were good people and that drinking wasn't a big deal. Getting drunk was fun, and I was unwilling to give up the attention I received when I went out.

However, I began to question my behavior. I started hanging out with Christian students who didn't participate in the party scene. I was torn. A part of me wanted to get out of the college chaos, but another part of me still was attracted to it. I began to oscillate between the two groups, trying to find out where I belonged.

I tried praying at times throughout this search, but none of it ever came from the heart. My prayer consisted of things I felt obligated to say to God. I'd either ask him for something he could do or ask him to forgive me for something I had done. It was difficult, because I didn't feel as if I even knew *how* to pray.

A New Beginning

Peter and I became very close, and we began dating. Like me, he was going through a conversion of sorts. He had left the Catholic Church in his adolescent years for evangelical Protestantism. Now he and his roommate, Dave, a very devout Catholic, had begun discussing the claims of the Catholic Church, and Peter was rethinking his beliefs. He was very excited by what he was discovering, and he spent a lot of time reading books about the history and teachings of the Church.

I was a little interested in the things Peter was learning. But to me the Catholic Church was still just another Christian "denomination."

One night Peter asked me to go out for coffee with Dave and him. He wanted to talk about the Church and answer some of the questions and objections I had been raising. I agreed, having no idea how much of an impact our conversation was going to have on my life.

After we had sat down at a table, Dave opened his Bible and began to read John 6, carefully explaining every line from a Catholic perspective. I couldn't believe what I was hearing. Everything he said about Jesus' real presence in the Eucharist seemed to make sense. By the time he finished his explanation, there were tears of joy in my eyes. The only words I could say were, "This is exactly what I have been looking for." Finally I had found the answer to the meaning of life.

After that night I joined Peter in his study of the Catholic Church. Everything I learned made sense to me, and I knew that there was no turning back. I had found my home, my place of peace.

I realized that God had not abandoned me during the traumatic accident with my friends. Though I had experienced profound suffering through it, that suffering couldn't compare to the suffering that my Lord endured for me, nor to his love.

Now I rejoice in the fact that I am alive. I try to live each day for God's honor and glory, and I receive my strength from the Body and Blood of his Son, our Lord Jesus Christ, in the Eucharist—in which all suffering finds its meaning.

TEN

Breaking Free[1]

David Prosen

My family consisted of my father, mother, my younger sister, Darlene, and me. My mother and I had a good relationship, but my father and I did not. An alcoholic, he often physically abused me. He tried to teach me the things that he enjoyed, such as carpentry and landscaping, but these efforts always ended with his losing patience, screaming obscenities and calling me names.

My dad never taught me anything about sports. At school, when it was time to divide into teams, I was one of the last picked. The team that ended up having me often complained loudly, making it clear that I was not like them.

Everything associated with masculinity made me panic. As a child I didn't enjoy playing with cars and toy guns. Instead I liked role-playing games like house and, yes, even dolls.

On the other hand I was attracted to males, and this attraction became sexual when I reached puberty. This brought me much turmoil. I hadn't asked for or chosen this attraction. It made me fear that my male peers were right: I was different and did not belong.

An older male befriended me when I was fifteen. I began to look up to him as an older brother. One night he betrayed this friendship by taking advantage of me sexually. For the next three months he played mind games with me and emotionally abused me. I sank into deep despair.

I then decided to give Jesus a chance. At first this decision gave me an emotional high, but despite my years of catechism classes, I didn't understand my faith or the sacraments. I didn't recognize the sustaining power of the real presence of Jesus in the Eucharist. When the emotional high left, I became very lonely, and I felt once again that I didn't fit in.

I began using marijuana and alcohol to help numb the pain. At the age of eighteen I went to my first gay bar. At first it was exhilarating; I felt as if I finally belonged somewhere. But the emptiness only worsened, and I relied even more heavily on substances to help deal with the pain.

I lived an active gay life for two years, during which I slept with about a hundred different men. I wasn't even trying to be promiscuous—at least not yet. I was trying to find someone to love me, and it wasn't happening.

I turned my life over to Christ several more times, still not understanding that conversion is an ongoing, daily process by which God's grace transforms us. I always would fall back into the bondage of sin and head deeper into darkness.

After one of these falls I learned of places where one could go to have anonymous sex. I so desperately wanted to be held and loved that I fell into a horrendous cycle of sexual addiction. I would fall into sin, feel worse, do it again to feel better, feel even worse and on and on. Looking back today, I have no idea how many men I was with sexually.

In the midst of all this pain, my sister, to whom I had become very close, suddenly collapsed with a heart attack and died. She was only twenty-one. After working through some of the grief, her death forced me to face my own mortality. I needed to work seriously at building a strong foundation on Christ, instead of looking for the emotional highs that I had depended on in the past.

A Roller Coaster Within

By God's grace some awesome things started happening. I quit alcohol and drugs and completely dropped out of the gay scene, remaining chaste for five and a half years. God helped me forgive my dad, and that relationship improved.

But I wasn't able to see these amazing things God was doing because I was trapped in my own shame. When I saw an attractive person, my heart might race, or I might feel butterflies in my stomach. I felt that these sensations could only mean that I was an evil and awful person. I begged God many times every day for a cure, but the attraction wouldn't go away.

Some people said, "You don't have enough faith." Others said, "You must be sinning in some other area of your life." These statements added to my shame.

Then a friend said, "David, maybe God isn't curing you because maybe there isn't anything wrong with being homosexual." After much thought I decided she might be right. I went back to a life of sin.

Now I believe that God used this imperfect situation to teach me some truths about what love really is. He never let go of me, even when I let go of him.

One day I felt him saying to my heart, "Yes, you never chose this attraction, but you *can* choose whether or not you will act on it."

I picked up the *Catechism of the Catholic Church* and read that homosexuality was a cross that some must bear (see *CCC*, 2357–2359). All Christians have to bear their crosses. "Jesus told his disciples, 'If any man would come after me, let him deny himself and take up his cross and follow me'" (Matthew 16:24). Jesus gives us the grace to carry our crosses; all we have to do is ask him and be open to these graces. If it weren't for crosses such as Darlene's death, I am sure that I would be spiritually and physically dead.

By God's grace I have been chaste for *over ten years now,* and this time there is no shame! Several years ago I enrolled at Franciscan University of Steubenville, and since then the Lord has been leading me on a journey of healing.

The Lord showed me that I was harboring anger toward the childhood male peers who mocked and teased me. I had transferred this anger to any male whom I perceived as being macho.

Further, in reading *The Battle for Normality* by Gerard J.M. Van Den Aardweg, I learned that the attraction I had toward males was actually an admiration of those who had masculine or physical traits that I felt I lacked as a child. In puberty this admiration became sexualized. I learned that when I was living the homosexual lifestyle, I was coveting what other men possessed. I thought I was affirmed as a man when men who were more masculine or more attractive than I showed an interest in me.

True love is not about seeking affirmation or attempting to have our physical and emotional needs met. As John Paul II stated in his *Theology of the Body,* love is a sincere gift of self, and God and others will meet our various needs when we express love in this authentic manner.

God has brought Catholic male friends into my life, and he has been helping me relate to men in healthy friendships. Two of these men spent time these past three years teaching me how to throw, catch and hit a baseball. I'm not excellent, but for the first time I have courage to play the game with others. My confidence has increased, and that child inside of me has been getting the affirmation he so desperately sought.

Grace-Filled Courage

One thing I found very helpful in my journey was my involvement with Courage, the only Catholic support group for those with same-sex attraction approved by the Catholic Church. Members of Courage strive to live chaste lives in accordance with the Church's teachings. John Paul

II called Courage "the work of God." When I attended my first National Courage Conference, I saw this played out as attendees shared their stories. I witnessed God's love, power and healing.

A person struggling with same-sex attraction is not alone. The Courage Web site (www.couragerc.net) is filled with articles, meeting information, recommended readings and opportunities for online support with other members.

Do I still struggle with same-sex attraction? Yes, but the attractions are less intense. As a result of the healing God has brought to my life, I am feeling things toward the opposite sex that I haven't felt before. I don't know what God's will is for me, but I want to remain open to whatever he has in mind, whether it is the chaste single life or marriage.

Some people told me that I had to be true to myself and accept my homosexuality in order to be happy. God has shown me that I am being true to myself by living in accordance with his Word. I am happier now than ever before. I no longer escape pain, but instead I try to work through it. And with each time comes growth. And with each growth comes a profound joy and peace in Jesus Christ.

ELEVEN

A Cold Day in Hell

Brad Gholston

My story is not an easy one to tell. In fact, I find it difficult even to reflect upon the key events surrounding my conversion. For although I was born into a Methodist family who instilled in me the importance of living a godly life, I spent the better part of my time seeking the glamour that the world has to offer—namely, *money*, *sex* and *power*.

As far back as I can remember, a large stature, an extremely short fuse and a penchant for getting into trouble without getting caught characterized me. The older I grew, the worse things became.

The worst part about it all was that I led a double life. Unless someone was directly involved in my "extracurricular activities," he or she probably thought that I was an upstanding guy. As a matter of fact, some people probably saw me as a role model for what a man of God should be like, since I was on the leadership council of my high school youth group.

I loved my life. Had anyone asked me in those days, I would have told them that it would be *a cold day in hell* before I would change my ways. But God had other plans for me. On July 21, 2000, the summer after my senior year in high school—the Jubilee Year—I had an *encounter* with Christ that transformed my life.

Jesus Calls

I was at a Protestant church camp, which I had been attending for several summers. The entire week unfolded in a completely familiar manner—that is, up until the last day, when we all went into a small chapel to have a worship service. It was your typical Protestant service, consisting of singing, testimonies and an altar call.

I had done it a thousand times before, but this time something was different. This time I actually felt guilt for my sins. For a brief moment God showed me a glimpse of my true self, and I was utterly disgusted with what I saw. Tears streamed down my face.

What is going on? I asked myself. My other side responded: *Snap out of it, Brad. You have a great life. You're going to play Division One football next year!*

In truth, however, I knew exactly what was going on. Christ was calling me to live for him and for his glory. I answered his call with a resounding *yes* and professed him as my personal Lord and Savior for the first time.

So that was it. *Hallelujah! I'm saved, and hell has frozen over!* Hardly. God was just getting started with me. Hell hadn't frozen over; it had just gotten some air-conditioning.

A good friend named Mark was the only Catholic I knew growing up. As fate would have it, Mark and his older brother had similar conversions on the same weekend as my experience at camp. You can imagine how surprised (and overjoyed) I was to learn of this when I returned home. God gave me an immediate brother with whom to pursue my faith journey. The two of us hit the ground running, and we spent the rest of the summer delving into Scripture and praising God at various Protestant worship services throughout the city.

At summer's end we both left for our respective colleges, knowing that we had a long and difficult road ahead of us. While I spent most of the following year in a three-step cycle of backsliding and repentance, followed by a short period of spiritual growth, Mark spent much of the year growing in his faith as a Catholic.

Then, one day in late February, I received a phone call that would change the course of my life. I vividly remember how surreal everything felt that Monday morning when I was told that Devaughn Darling, one of my closest childhood friends, had died during an off-season football workout at one of the nation's top football schools. In an instant my faith was shattered, and my life spiraled into an abyss of confusion, doubt and questions. *How could God have allowed this? Did he even exist?*

I immediately began searching for answers by looking both into other faiths and more deeply into my own. I concluded that the one true God resided in the Christian faith, the only religion that professed Jesus Christ to be Lord. But where within Christianity could the truth be found? There were so many different beliefs and denominations. I had to search deeper.

I believed that my only hope for finding an answer was to get lost in Scripture. And it wasn't long before I came across Matthew 16:18: "And I tell you, you are Peter, and on this rock I will build my Church, and the gates of Hades shall not prevail against it."

Finally I had found a clue! After pondering it for several days, I concluded that if Jesus had founded a church, then that was where I wanted to be—assuming it still existed. Thus I began to research the historical roots and beliefs of most of the mainstream Protestant denominations, hoping to find the "one true Church" that Jesus himself had established.

The Deepest Root

Not long after I began my study, I told Mark about the journey I had embarked upon. That's when he posed the question: "What about Catholicism; have you looked into that?"

I responded with a sheepish *no*. There couldn't be any truth in Catholicism, could there? However, by this point my faith was so uncertain that I figured I might as well give it a shot.

To my surprise I quickly discovered that almost every history book that I read considered Catholicism to be the oldest "denomination." This broke down my wall of prejudice against Catholicism.

I returned to my native Houston that summer, eager to resume my search for the truth with Mark. I found out that his mother had purchased a set of videos entitled *Catholic Adult Education on Video.* Mark gently urged me to begin watching them with him, and with my new openness to the Catholic faith, I agreed.

What followed over the next three months was a process of prayer and study, with the guidance of the Holy Spirit, that worked to lead me home. The video information challenged me with biblical and historical evidence for the reasonableness of the Catholic faith. Mark lovingly guided me along the path to the fullness of the truth. Many providential events demolished the walls of doubt and objection that surrounded my heart. One by one I came to believe each of the doctrines that set the Catholic Church apart.

One day Mark asked me where I stood in relation to Catholicism and what I intended to do. I unwittingly responded that I believed in all that the Church taught and professed to be true, but I didn't think that I would convert. I will never forget his response: "But, Brad, just remember, failure to give full obedience is really just disobedience."

This struck my very core. Mark was right. That Easter I was confirmed and received into the Church. I don't know if hell has frozen over, but I know that I have found my home.

Since that time I have grown in my relationship with the Lord. No longer do I see myself as a descendant of Adam but rather as an adopted son of God. My heavenly

Father loves me so much that he desires that I share in his own divine life, that I partake in his divine nature.

It was God's grace that changed my life. I am thankful for Mark and other wonderful friends who were instrumental along the way. Unworthy as I am, I now enjoy the ultimate gift of feasting at my Father's table.

TWELVE

My Road to Rome

Jim Lee

My journey to Catholicism was like the disciples' journey to Emmaus: It was an unexpected encounter with the Lord. As their eyes were opened in the breaking of the bread, so mine were opened at the table of the Mass (see Luke 24:13–32). Little did I know that my road to Emmaus would be my road to Rome!

My journey began in high school, where I met a Catholic girl who knew both her faith and Scripture. I was a Bible-quoting Protestant, born and raised Presbyterian. When I met this Catholic woman who could articulate her beliefs and who knew the Lord, I realized that the views I had of Catholicism were misconceptions.

One day this friend invited me to attend a prayer meeting at her house. The plan was to pray the rosary. I didn't think it could hurt, and I was intrigued to see what it was all about.

Admittedly, I was freaked out by my initial experience with the rosary! Nevertheless, I saw firsthand that Catholics did not worship Mary but rather asked for her intercession, much as a friend would ask me for mine. Through this prayer group I began to learn about many other Catholic beliefs. The people there gave me countless books, tapes and documents explaining the faith. Though I disagreed on many issues, I developed a deep respect for Catholicism.

The Bread of Life

There was one doctrine that challenged my faith, pricked my conscience and began an interior conflict that would last for years: the doctrine of the Holy Eucharist.

I was shocked the first time I read the famous "Bread of Life" passage in John 6 from a Catholic perspective. As a Protestant, I believed that Jesus was "spiritually" present in Communion but that the elements remained bread and wine. Communion for me was merely a sign of spiritual union. It blew my mind to learn that Catholics believed that Christ was present Body, Blood, soul and divinity in the Eucharist.

What startled me even more was the command Jesus gave to receive him in this way: "Unless you eat the flesh of the Son of man and drink his blood, you have no life in you" (John 6:53). It was comforting to learn that I wasn't the only one who had difficulty with this teaching: some of Jesus' disciples declared, "This is a hard saying; who can listen to it?" (v. 60).

Jesus' response was simple but clear. "Do you take offense at this? Then what if you were to see the Son of man ascending where he was before?" (John 6:61–62). His answer was, essentially, "Take it or leave it! If you can't accept this, you can't accept all of my teachings."

In fact, many of Jesus' disciples did decide to leave, after which he turned to the twelve and asked if they too would abandon him. He was ready to lose all of his followers for the sake of this truth. But Peter declared, "Lord, to whom shall we go? You have the words of eternal life" (John 6:68).

This teaching was an earth-shattering one for me. If it was not true, Catholics were committing the most grievous sin of idolatry imaginable. If it was true, it demanded my greatest devotion, humility and obedience. It meant that the Lord I had come to know and love was present Body, Blood, soul and divinity at every Catholic Mass!

I brought this Eucharist question with me to the University of Notre Dame in the fall of 2000. There I continued to pursue my interest in Catholicism.

Though I was a pre-med major, I discovered a new academic love in theology, and I began researching the faith with an even greater intensity. I became enamored with the rich tradition of the Church, from Augustine to Aquinas to John Paul II. I took a particular interest in the early Church and began reading the works of Justin Martyr, Ambrose, Augustine and many others.

Through my studies I discovered a deep and wonderful continuity of faith. This was particularly evident regarding Holy Communion. Century after century the Fathers affirmed and reaffirmed Christ's real presence in the Blessed Sacrament. They were unwilling to compromise on the reality of his Body and Blood at the Holy Sacrifice of the altar.

I began to assent intellectually to this truth, yet my heart resisted. *How could the Lord of the universe come to us under the forms of bread and wine? How could I have been unaware of this my whole life?* This was an entirely different understanding of reality. My world had been turned upside down.

Courage to Believe

Despite my difficulties I was captivated by the liturgy. Amazed that Catholics could go to church seven days a week, I began to attend daily Mass. If what they claimed was actually true—that they were receiving the real presence of Jesus in Communion—nothing could keep me away! I spent many hours in a chapel, asking Jesus if he was really there. I had to know the truth. Was Jesus truly present in every Catholic Church, everywhere in the world? I marveled at this incredible gift that Catholics enjoyed.

The Lord began to work in me. He gave me a deep desire to receive him at Mass. Like the disciples on the road to Emmaus, my heart burned while I was in his presence. Though I still fought this desire with all my might, I longed to receive my Lord, in humility and truth.

A friend of mine told me about a prayer: "Lord, grant me the grace to know your truth, the courage to act on it and the humility to live it." I adopted this as my own.

One weekend some of my friends planned a trip to Chicago to hear Scott Hahn speak on his book *The Lamb's*

Supper. I had read several of Dr. Hahn's books already and found them very helpful, so I jumped at the chance to ask him my Eucharist question.

After the talk I asked the former Presbyterian, "How could it be bread and wine for you one day and the next day the body and blood of Christ?"

He looked at me intently and asked: "If you can believe that Jesus Christ—a thirty-three-year-old Nazarene Jew, the son of a carpenter—was the Son of God, what is bread and wine to God?"

His point was clear and compelling. The great mystery of Christianity is the Incarnation—the fact that Jesus Christ was God and man. This truth displays God's limitless power and love. If Jesus is Lord, then his words are truth, even if they scandalize us. We must say yes to him, no matter what the cost.

After reading John 6 for the hundredth time, I knew the Lord was speaking directly to me. He was calling me home to the Catholic Church. This call was a personal invitation to receive him as he willed—completely and totally—on his terms, not my own. My heart was finally ready.

This meant walking away from the Protestant church I loved and risking alienation from my family. Yet I realized that conversion to Catholicism was not a rejection of my Protestant faith but rather its perfect fulfillment.

I began the Rite of Christian Initiation for Adults after having attended daily Mass for nearly two years. When I entered the Catholic Church on March 3, 2002, and received the Blessed Sacrament for the first time, I encountered the same Jesus Christ the disciples had encountered some two thousand years ago in the "breaking of the bread." I didn't enter just the Catholic Church; I entered the heavenly presence of my Lord and Savior here on earth.

Like the disciples on the road to Emmaus, I recognized Jesus in the breaking of the bread. And also like them, my heart burned with joy.

THIRTEEN

Fully Alive

Father Quinn Mann

God, what do you want me to do with my life?"

This question, which had plagued me for years, was finally answered during the Jubilee Year of 2000—the year that abundant graces flowed through the Church. I had had enough of a joyless life. I was tired of just living instead of being fully alive. So at the age of twenty-four, I stood up on Easter Sunday morning and declared to my family: "I'm going to become a Roman Catholic priest!"

The youngest of five children, I was the only one who had been raised Catholic. At one time I had considered attending a high school seminary. However, when I discovered that the seminary didn't have a football team, I opted out and began a journey away from the Lord and his Church. I did the typical high school things—sports, working, dating and getting into trouble—but God's call kept persisting in spite of my best efforts to ignore it.

I worked at a marina for six years, and I frequently became involved in intense conversations with an atheist coworker named Pete. After one heated theological discussion, Pete was quiet for a while before making a startling exclamation: "Quinn, you should be a %*# priest!" I couldn't believe what I was hearing. Even an atheist could see that I was called!

Sadly, however, I chose to ignore the call, and my life in college didn't differ all that much from my life in high school. Seldom did I attend church. I worked a ton, partied hard and dated as much as possible. All of these things helped me to ignore the fact that God was calling me to something special.

Things slowly began to change during my senior year of college. I was invited to serve as a water ski and wake board instructor at a Christian camp north of Seattle. There I was exposed to an entirely new group of people: young adults on fire for Jesus Christ. A group of evangelical Protestants ran the camp—I was the only Catholic there—and I was both challenged and stretched by the experience. It forced me to interact with the faith of others and subsequently to reexamine my relationship to my own faith.

Around this time I was involved in a serious relationship with a woman I had known throughout college. I thought she was the one. She was a committed evangelical. We had many discussions about our faith, and I eventually decided to leave the Catholic Church and become a non-denominational Christian.

In spite of our mutual commitment to the Lord, the relationship became very unhealthy. I was using her, and she was using me. Before we knew it we were practically living together. We knew what we were doing was wrong, though the culture told us it was fine and normal.

Finally, burdened with guilt and shame, I went to confession and laid it all out. When I was done I felt as if the weight of all my sin had been lifted off my shoulders. I began to spend time in front of the Blessed Sacrament, and it was there that God revealed his true presence to me. There was no running from him any longer.

I tried to share my experience with my girlfriend. I told her that Jesus was really present in the Eucharist.

"Euch-a-what?" she asked, confused.

Soon we were debating about the essential truths of the Christian faith. She took the Protestant perspective; I took the Catholic. I began to read various Christian books, both Catholic and Protestant, and I realized I was convinced about the truth of the Catholic faith. Although I tried to explain the love and the joy I had found, my girlfriend couldn't see what I saw. We drifted apart, and I eventually called off the relationship.

I had found life, and I was excited. I moved out of my apartment and began living in a church rectory with a compassionate priest. Lent that year was my most penitential Lent ever! I renounced everything I had worked so hard to achieve: money, marriage, my business marketing dreams. All of these things became inconsequential to my calling.

What struck me the most was the realization that I really wasn't losing anything; in fact, I was gaining everything! I discovered that being fully alive means honestly answering the question I had been avoiding: "What does

God want me to do with my life?" It was only through discovering God's will for the life *he* gave me that I was able to move beyond "just getting by" to being fully alive in him.

The following summer I hooked up with a Catholic group who traveled around the country sharing the love of Christ with young people. It was truly a missionary experience, and it helped prepare me for the five long years of seminary formation that lay ahead. For it was at the doors of a major Catholic seminary that I found myself at the end of August 2001. I still had "pavement under my fingernails" because God had to drag me to this place, but I was at peace. And I was grateful for his love and grace.

Seminary had its challenges, but God continued to transform my life and bring me closer to him. I stand in awe of the tremendous gift the Church has given me and other young priests: the opportunity to be formed into holy men who seek Christ in all we do.

Now I couldn't be happier. It is humbling to proclaim the truth of Christ every day and everywhere. Of course, new challenges will develop, but I have an overwhelming sense of peace about my life. I know that there isn't anything I can't do without the help of God. He is good, he is in control, and he will *never* be outdone in generosity.

FOURTEEN

Cradle Convert

Kelly Franklin

My conversion to the Catholic Church is not my fault. God handed it to me—pure and simple—as a gift.

I was an "MK"—a missionary kid—born and raised as an evangelical Protestant Christian. At age four I asked Jesus Christ to come into my heart and be my personal Lord and Savior. I still have the leather-bound King James Version of the New Testament that my parents gave me to celebrate the occasion. At age eight I asked to be baptized as a statement of my membership in the body of Christ; and baptized I was, "Jesus style," in a river by a Costa Rican Baptist minister.

Why did I do these things? Because they made sense. My parents told me about Jesus, heaven and baptism, and I believed them. Simple as that. Too young to really read or understand the Bible, I was already trusting in the "tradition" of my trustworthy elders. *Sola scriptura*, the Protestant doctrine of "the Bible alone," was already out the window.

My family spent the next two years in Guatemala, where I attended a Christian missionary school. Our ignorance of the Catholic Church was staggering. My parents admit today that they had moved to a mostly Catholic country to evangelize the people without knowing anything about Catholicism. I remember a third-grade classmate who archly informed me that Catholics went around with black crosses on their foreheads all the time; it was a mental image that stuck with me.

Looking back now, I realize that much of our faith was unsure. Where did the Bible come from? Why do so many Christians simply agree to disagree? What about things like baptism, the end times and the myriad and contradictory private interpretations of the Scriptures—all claiming to be guided by the Holy Spirit? Needless to say, there was a lot of gray area, a lot of church-hopping and a lot of questions that one didn't ask.

Fast forward to our return to the United States in 1995. My relationship with God was fair for a fifth-grader: I had vague notions of private prayer and of the Bible but no real consciousness of sin, grace or Church history. My parents put my sister Jody and me in a Catholic elementary school because it was similar to our missionary school in Guatemala. At this point my parents were learning about Church history and exploring the idea of Christian liturgy, but we were nowhere near entering the Catholic Church— or so we thought.

At the Catholic elementary school I learned Catholic prayers, including the rosary, and attended weekly Mass without receiving Communion. I was attracted to the formality and the reverence of ritual prayer, as well as intrigued by the old chipped statuary of the saints in the crypt of the church. I liked the many outward signs of Catholic spirituality—something to capture a fifth-grade boy's short attention span—crossing myself, genuflecting, bowing, using respectful titles for priests and nuns.

Strangely enough, I longed for such outward signs even at this young age. I wanted to *do* something to worship God. *Worship* to me connoted the prostration, bowing, incense and ceremony that we read about in the Old Testament. We worship the same God as Abraham did, and I wanted to *feel* as if I was worshiping.

Much later I would read and understand James 2:24: "not by faith alone" are we justified. I realize now that God, in his mercy, allows us to participate in his saving work through "good works" and the physical acts of piety and worship. But at the time these were just the half-conscious musings of an eleven-year-old.

Unbeknownst to me, my parents were wrestling with their growing knowledge and love of the Catholic faith. I distinctly remember the moment my dad sat me down to explain to me the real presence of Christ in the Eucharist.

"Kelly," he said, "remember when I told you that the communion we used to receive in church was just a symbol and a commemoration of the Lord's Supper?"

Sensing where the conversation was going, I felt an accusation welling up in my chest. But my dad beat me to it. "I was wrong," he said simply. I will never forget his humility.

Jesus Christ really meant what he said at the Last Supper: "This is my body" (Luke 22:19). My parents wanted to take God at his word.

That Easter, in 1995, near the end of my fifth-grade year, my whole family entered the Catholic Church at the Vigil Mass. I remember the smell of the holy chrism with which my parents were confirmed. I remember the Irish priest who welcomed us into the Church and gave us Holy Communion—the Body and Blood of Christ.

When we returned home I didn't feel any different. I had no idea of the full implications of my newfound faith, of how much God's Church would demand of me and offer me. I was like a newborn baby, completely unaware of the laughter, the sweat, the triumphs and the failures ahead. God doesn't tell us all the joys and sorrows that will follow from our trusting him. As he did for the fishermen in the Gospel, he just asks us to "put out into the deep" (Luke 5:4).

My favorite author, Flannery O'Connor, wrote: "What one has as a born Catholic is something given and accepted before it is experienced."[1] Converting at a young age as I did, her statement rings true for me. I accepted the truths of the Church just as a child accepts the reality of gravity before knowing Newton's laws.

I live in wonder at the nonstop unfolding of God's divine plan for me. His Church, given to me before I could realize the full value of it, has uplifted, sanctified and radically changed my life. My matter-of-fact assent to my family's conversion to Catholicism has given beauty and order to every facet of my life. The sacraments have strengthened me through the years. The Eucharist in particular has pervaded my studies, my relationships, my joy, my sadness, my suffering. Nothing has remained untouched by Jesus Christ, and everything he touches blossoms.

My journey to Christ was a gift, and so is yours. It's up to us what we do with that gift.

FIFTEEN

Nowhere Else to Go

Peter Ericksen

I hated going to my sixth-grade Confraternity of Christian Doctrine (CCD) classes. The Bibles we used were falling apart, and the workbooks were full of lame pictures from the 1970s. There is only one word that can describe the experience: boring! I never learned anything. And to make matters worse, the classes were scheduled during *Monday Night Football.*

Fortunately, I didn't have to endure the agony all by myself. My childhood best friend, Derek, was also in the class. Derek was one of the most talented and caring people I knew. He could throw a football farther than anyone else, and yet he was always sticking up for the less popular kids. Derek made CCD bearable. Little did I know that very shortly I would have to face CCD—and life itself—without him. Derek was in a serious accident and fell into a coma.

I was devastated. Never before had I questioned the meaning—and goodness—of life. One night after class I fled to the church and positioned myself directly in front of the life-sized crucifix that hung behind the altar. I stared up at the large, dark hanging figure. "Why, why Derek?"

My best friend was in a coma, and I blamed the man on the cross. I couldn't understand. "Come off that cross and save yourself," I prayed, "and Derek."

My friend eventually came out of the coma, but he wasn't the same. This left me with other questions.

Jesus Is Lord!

My first major conversion came in high school. My main priorities at that time were wrestling and girls. My high school best friend shared these priorities but added a third: Matt was a devoted Christian. And through his persistent coercion, I eventually consented to attend a Christian camp with him one summer.

The week was great. I had loads of fun, made tons of friends and met plenty of girls. Throughout the week we heard inspiring talks from a powerful speaker. His message was simple: God has a plan for our lives, but sin causes us to turn from his plan. Because of sin, many abandon the love of our heavenly Father for a life that leads to self-destruction.

These words pierced my heart. In an instant I was back in sixth grade, reflecting on what had happened to Derek and asking God about the meaning of life.

I learned that there was only one man in all of history who had lived a sinless life: Jesus Christ—the Son of God, the anointed one. It was Jesus who took upon himself the sin of humanity and offered up his own life on a cross. I could almost hear him say, "This is my love for you. Come, receive me."

So I did. One night at that Christian camp, I invited Jesus to be my personal Savior and Lord.

For the next six years I was a fired-up, nondenominational, evangelical Christian, and I attended a vibrant community church in a nearby city. The only thing that mattered to me was Jesus. I also became a firm believer in the sixteenth-century Protestant formula, *sola scriptura* ("by Scripture alone"). After all, the church was assembled around the Bible. Wherever there was Scripture, there was the church.

My fervor continued into my college years. I attended a Catholic college, where I was active in bringing many wonderful Protestant groups to campus, such as Campus Crusade for Christ and InterVarsity. It wasn't an easy walk; my faith was challenged on more than one occasion.

One of my religious studies professors took great delight in separating the "Jesus of history" from the "Christ of faith," thus "deconstructing" the biblical witness. He taught us, for example, that there is no "biblical position" on the issue of homosexuality. Even though I didn't agree with his conclusion, his arguments shook me up. I was forced to rethink my understanding of biblical authority.

Ironically, my faith was also challenged in my experience at various nondenominational churches. I was surprised at how churches—even those from similar, Bible-based perspectives—could be completely different in almost everything they did and believed. I realized that I had preferences when it came to styles of worship.

How can I prefer one church to another? I wondered. *Aren't we all Christian? Don't we all go by the Bible?*

These questions were accentuated when I witnessed a Catholic friend of mine getting berated while visiting a Protestant church: "Catholics worship Mary." "Catholics believe they can work their way into heaven." "Catholics believe they sacrifice Christ on the altar." "Catholics believe that they get a second chance when they die and go to purgatory." Her rather unpleasant encounter didn't sit well me. I had been away from the Catholic Church for a long time, but I wasn't about to reject Catholicism in its entirety.

Catholic Questions

Later that year I was fortunate enough to attend a large Christian youth rally. It was an incredible experience. I prayed with two thousand passionate Christians from all sorts of denominational backgrounds and spoke at length with many of them. I loved it.

One night a few of us guys were hanging out in our hotel room, playing guitar and talking about faith. Somehow the Catholic Church came up in the conversation. One guy said, "I used to be Catholic, *but then* I met Jesus and accepted him as my personal Lord and Savior." Within minutes the guys were naming all of the "false Catholic teachings": things like Mass, purgatory, papacy and, of course, Mary.

Not quite sure how to respond, I tried defending Catholicism: "I grew up Catholic, and I don't remember learning that Catholics worship Mary. I'm pretty sure they don't." I couldn't offer any further explanation, and the guys promptly rejected my input.

Before the rally was over, I had made a list of "Catholic questions" I wanted answered. As soon as I arrived back home, I picked up the phone and called Arch, the only faithful Catholic I knew at the time. I was certain he could help me work through these issues.

It was the middle of the night, but I told Arch we needed to talk "now!" He came over, and I went through my list point by point: "Why do Catholics put priests on pedestals?" "What *is* purgatory?" "Why do you believe Mary was conceived without sin; wasn't Christ the only sinless person to walk the earth?" "Why do you have a pope?"

Finally, around three in the morning, I challenged Arch to show me where the Church derived her belief in the real presence of Christ in the Eucharist. If the real presence could be found *in the Bible*, I was prepared to give in on Mary and purgatory. *After all,* I thought to myself, *if Catholics have* this *right, then what else really matters?*

Arch opened up the Scriptures to John 6:25–71. He read it and then asked me some simple yet powerful questions to help me understand how Catholics interpret this passage: "Why do the Jewish followers reject Jesus' teaching? What about it made them leave? If Jesus' words weren't literal, then why did he say that this bread is his flesh (verses 51–56)? Why did he say that we must really *eat* his flesh?"

It was incredible. I had never studied this passage before, and I was compelled by what I saw.

When we came to verse 66—where many of Jesus' disciples abandoned him because of this difficult teaching—I felt as if Jesus was asking me the same question he posed to the remaining twelve apostles in the following verse: "Will you also go away?"

I couldn't deny it any longer. I had no other place to go.

God so loved the world that he sent his only begotten Son—Jesus Christ—to give himself for us (John 3:16). And Jesus hasn't *stopped* giving himself to us. Through the Holy Sacrifice of the Mass, we can truly receive Christ in the most intimate way. But this sacred act requires eyes of faith.

When I was a Protestant, I invited Jesus Christ to come into *my* life. And now—at each and every Mass—Jesus Christ invites me to enter into *his* divine life through the Eucharist.

I once believed that the Church was built around the Bible. I now know that the Church is assembled around the Bible *and* the Body and Blood of Christ, as Vatican Council II stated: "In all legitimate local congregations \…the faithful are gathered by the preaching of Christ's Gospel and the mystery of the Lord's Supper is celebrated, 'so that through the Body and Blood of the Lord the whole brotherhood is united.'"[1]

Wherever the Eucharist is, there is the eternally young Catholic Church. Even more than entering our life, Christ wants us to enter into his.

SIXTEEN

Mending Broken Boundaries

Katie

I grew up Catholic and never spent a significant period of time away from the Church. I had a wonderful childhood. I was loved and cared for, and I had wonderful teachers to guide me on my way through life—the most important being my parents.

Due to my dad's job, our family had to relocate about every three years. While I knew that this was a "different" lifestyle, I never thought negatively of it. Every move was a chance to meet new friends and explore new places.

I figured my insecurities were normal. The voices of the seventh-grade girls who had called me names occasionally echoed in my mind, but for the most part I was able to rise above their hurtful words and focus on my positive qualities. I knew I would never win the Miss America Pageant, but I also knew people loved me for who I was.

I always had a date for dances and was involved in four romantic relationships during high school. I had a passion for children and found great joy in helping others. I was an active volunteer in many community programs. I did well in school and looked forward to college. I pursued a deeper understanding of my faith, joined our church's youth group and became a peer minister.

My first two years of college were quite enjoyable. I was developing lifelong friendships, growing intellectually and continuing my journey of faith. I was fortunate enough to attend a Catholic university, where men and women who shared a passion for the Catholic faith surrounded me. I attended daily Mass, went to confession regularly and experienced the peace that comes from spending time with Jesus in the Blessed Sacrament.

I became a resident advisor during my junior year of college. It was an amazing opportunity to offer help to others as they adjusted to college life. Unfortunately, however, I became so distracted by day-to-day activities that I began to let my prayer life slide and spend less time with my faith-filled friends. I blamed my negligence on the extra time and energy required of a resident assistant.

Numerous conversations with the girls in my dorm exposed me to the suffering that is a part of so many lives. I didn't think it was fair that God gave me a life of blessing while others seemed to experience constant pain: sexual abuse, eating disorders, neglect, suicidal tendencies, depression—the list went on. Something deep inside me began to doubt the goodness of God.

I had always known that there were problems in the world, but it wasn't until they were this close to me that I began to wonder, *When will my time come? When will God dump suffering on me?*

My questions and confusion slowly transformed into anger, and this led me to do the unthinkable: I prayed that God would let me fall away from him. I needed proof that he loved me, and I wondered if he would bring me back. I wanted to test him.

Temptation and Trial

At first I didn't take any special notice of her; she was just another woman in my dorm. But eventually we found ourselves spending the majority of our time together. I would listen intently as she described her painful struggle with depression. We would take walks through the city and let our problems fade into the night air. We would share stories from our past and discuss controversial issues of the present. I had found my best friend.

At this point in my life, I had made the decision to save sex for marriage. And by God's grace I had remained faithful to myself and my future husband. However, I paid little attention to boundaries in my friendships with women. Spooning and snuggling were common among many of us, marking only innocent, shared affection. Things changed one day when my best friend said, "I think I might be *in love* with you."

I can't describe how it felt to hear those words for the first time. I calmly answered, "If being in love means you care about someone and want to know more about that person, then I'm probably in love with you, too."

The next few months were a blur. We shared a first kiss. She brought me breakfast in bed and showered my room with balloons to celebrate a successful interview. We traveled together and accompanied each other to class. We would squeeze out the last seconds of every day just to spend one more moment in each other's company. Not once were we at peace with what we did behind closed doors. My family and friends likely had their suspicions, but I never told them about what was happening.

This was not what I wanted for my life. I cannot recall how many times I went to confession for our sin. I sought spiritual direction and resolved over and over again to discontinue what we were doing. Weekly we would discuss the possibility of just being friends again, and weekly we would fail.

I was torn. I became angry with God for allowing this to happen. I even tried convincing myself that everything was OK and that we could have a happy life together. I wrestled with the Church's teaching on homosexuality, and I cursed my conscience for not letting me be at peace with this relationship. Nothing made sense.

Even after I graduated from college and moved away, we still found ways to see each other. We continually resolved to maintain our friendship and to work as hard as necessary to keep the sin away. We had temporary successes, but we also experienced many failures.

A Cross to Bear

They say that "time heals all wounds." However, I prefer to say that "in time *God* heals all wounds." Through the loving support of friends and spiritual directors, and ultimately the abundant grace of God, the woman and I decided that we could no longer share in each other's lives. I had come to realize that our friendship was causing more pain than joy. By refusing to let God shape us as he desired, we were inhibiting growth in both of our lives.

We have been able to maintain this separation, but it has not been easy. It is *only* by the grace of God that I don't give in to my desire to call her on the phone or to send her a quick e-mail. I often wonder what and how she is doing these days. I dream of eventually being able to have a back-yard barbecue with our future families—of being able to enjoy the peace of each other's company again. Yet I know that our decision to let go of the friendship is for our good. This gives me peace, and I am beginning to heal.

Our society is very confused in its understanding of homosexuality. Popular television shows, news stories and other sources bombard us with distorted views of human sexuality. I can share my story now only because I have dealt with my confusion in this experience. There were many days when I asked myself, "Am I gay?" All signs seemed to indicate "yes," but I couldn't quite wrap my mind around it.

While I don't know if this cross will continue to be a part of my life, I know that I am responsible for what I do with it. Just because I have feelings—and even acted on those feelings in the past—does not mean that I have to be enslaved to them. The course is difficult, but I know God's grace is sufficient to liberate me from the shackles of sin.

"We are more than conquerors through him who loved us" (Romans 8:37).

I have met others who have had similar struggles; the problem is more common than I once thought. If you are struggling with this, please know that I pray for you daily. If you know someone who is struggling, please don't stop encouraging him or her to seek faithful guidance from a trusted priest or faithful counselor.

And pray. God hears and answers all prayers. "Ask, and it will be given you; seek, and you will find; knock, and it will be opened to you" (Matthew 7:7).

SEVENTEEN

From Belief to Love

Erin Hanson

I've always believed in God, but I haven't always loved him.

During the first six years of my life, I attended church every Sunday with my dad (the pastor), my mom and my older brother. Then my dad left the ministry, became a lawyer and moved us from Florida to Arizona.

I adapted pretty well to the changes, but they were a bit harder for my parents. The biggest challenge was to find a church they really liked. We started out visiting a different church every Sunday, but as the task became harder, we stopped attending church completely. My parents still taught me about God and Jesus, and I always believed in God and said prayers before bed at night.

Heartbreak

Things began to change as I got older. During my sophomore year of high school, I transferred to a new school and began hanging out with a group of friends who could be classified as "the wrong crowd."

My grandpa, with whom I had been very close, died that year. I was heartbroken. I never had the chance to say good-bye. I lay in bed many nights crying because I missed him but also because I was angry with God. *How could he let this happen?*

I decided that I was done with God. I decided to stop praying. My life changed—and not for the better.

I kept hanging out with my new friends, and I started dating the captain of the wrestling team. Now I had cool friends and a popular boyfriend. What else did I need? I began to ditch classes on a daily basis, and my grades quickly dropped.

This was the beginning of the darkest time of my life. My relationship with my boyfriend became increasingly unhealthy. I began to distrust him because he would lie to me about various things. I was hurt but too scared to leave the relationship for fear that my friends would think I was dumb and that no other guy would want to date me.

I began lying to my parents with great frequency. I was suspended from school for fighting. Before that I had never been sent to the principal's office, so my suspension came as a shock to many people—my parents especially. I knew I had let them down, and this troubled me greatly. I always had wanted to make them proud, and I was failing miserably. The guilt and shame were overwhelming, and my heart was broken again.

Right around this time my older brother converted to Catholicism. He kept inviting me to a Sunday night "youth group thing," but I always turned him down. Then I came to a point where I was willing to try anything that could help me feel better about myself. I agreed to go to the youth group meeting with him.

All I remember about that evening is the relief I felt in doing something that I didn't have to feel bad about. I didn't have to lie to my parents about where I was going, and I didn't return home feeling guilty. It was a truly liberating experience.

I began attending the youth group on a regular basis. Then I began to realize that my life needed to change. I had to stop hanging out with my friends. I had to stop skipping classes. And difficult as it was, I had to break up with my boyfriend.

The guy didn't understand what had changed, and he didn't understand what was wrong with our relationship. I had tried to explain the issues to him many times, but it was apparent that we were on two completely different paths. Telling him that I couldn't see him anymore was the right thing to do, but again I found myself heartbroken.

I felt very alone during this period of my life. I didn't talk to my friends at school anymore, and I hadn't been attending church long enough to make any close friends there. I remember hearing the words to a Jennifer Knapp song that described so perfectly what I was feeling: "And I know they are wrong when they say I am strong as the darkness covers me."[1] That was me. On the outside I looked fine, but on the inside everything was dark and broken.

By God's grace I was able to persevere through this lonely time. I kept going to Mass on Sundays with my brother, and I made many friends at church. It took time, but there was something about these new friendships that was worth the time and the effort. That "something" was Jesus.

The people at church had the kindness of Jesus in their eyes, his gentleness in their voice and his love in their hearts. At first they seemed unreal, but as time went on, I saw that they were the most real people I had ever met. I was reintroduced to Jesus at this point, and slowly but surely I began coming out of the darkness. I was becoming more of the person I had always wanted to be. I was beginning to recognize myself again.

Heartburn

Eventually I was faced with a difficult question: Did I really want to become Catholic? I had been attending Mass for about a year without taking part in the sacraments, and I had many questions about the faith.

My brother and I debated about numerous topics concerning Catholicism. Even though I didn't show it, my heart always burned after our discussions. I never wanted to admit that I was wrong, but the things my brother said sounded right. His words spoke to my heart, and I knew I had to make a decision.

I was scared. What would my parents think? Remember, my dad used to be a Protestant minister! But with each passing day Jesus kept calling me closer and closer to him, and I knew that if I wanted to be as close to Jesus as my heart desired, then I needed to become Catholic. So I did. And to my surprise, my parents were amazingly supportive.

On Easter Vigil, 2002—as a senior in high school—I was baptized and confirmed, and I received my first Holy Communion. Never before had my heart felt as joyful as it did that night. I was finally able to participate in the fullness of the Mass. Everything felt complete. I had become what I had been longing for ever since sophomore year: a new person. God found me when I was broken and lonely. He called me out of darkness and gave me the chance to start all over again.

Later that year I was blessed to attend Pope John Paul II's last World Youth Day in Toronto, Canada. I remember gathering for the opening Mass on the day we arrived. I stopped to look around at all the people. Thousands and thousands were there from all over the world; the crowds seemed to go on forever. It was then that I remembered something my brother had told me during one of our heated debates: The word *catholic* means "universal." I finally understood what my brother had meant.

I was speechless. I couldn't believe that God loved me so much that he called me to be a part of something so beautiful. This was huge, and somehow God had led me here. Words cannot describe the excitement that I felt then and continue to feel now.

Our God is a God of hope and love. He promises all of us a new life—no matter what our background—if only we let him love us. And he always keeps his promises.

EIGHTEEEN

Indissoluble Love

Christopher Graham

Everything that I am and every good that I possess come completely and utterly from the unmerited grace of Jesus Christ.

As I look at the path my life has taken, I am struck by the profound reality of this statement. The only response that I can have to his goodness is humble gratitude: gratitude for the richness of his mercy and for that particular grace of communion with his mystical body, the one, holy, Catholic and apostolic Church.

I remember very clearly the moment I first accepted Christ. I was five years old, and I was watching a Protestant evangelist on TV. He said that if I prayed with him to invite Christ into my heart, I would live forever with God in heaven. Sounded like a pretty good deal. I prayed in front of the television and went upstairs, firmly convinced that I had my own "little Jesus" living in my heart.

My parents were proud. At the time they were both nominally Christian. My grandpa is a very humble and kind Presbyterian pastor, and my sister and I grew up learning about the Christian faith. But for some reason a lot of what we learned at church did not seem to make much of a difference in our home.

Where Grace Abounds

It took a disaster for my family to come to grips with the reality of the gospel. During my junior year of high school—about two years after I started getting serious about my faith in Christ—infidelity on both sides threatened to tear my parents' marriage apart. Satan seemed to be scoring his final blow against my family, and its destruction appeared inevitable. For my sister and me, the safety and happiness we had known growing up in what many people had called the "perfect family" seemed to be lost forever.

I knew that my parents' marriage was indissoluble. God had bound them together as one in a mystical union, and no divorce document could reverse that. I knew this straight from Scripture: "Whoever divorces his wife and marries another, commits adultery against her; and if she divorces her husband and marries another, she commits adultery" (Mark 10:11–12).

It would have been easy for my parents to give up on one another, but God refused to give up on our family, and his undeserved grace made all the difference. As the light of hope grew dimmer and dimmer and was about to disappear, it exploded in a flash of divine grace.

My parents decided to try counseling. At first their motivation stemmed not so much from a spirit of reconciliation as from a desire to be able to say that they had "tried everything." But in the very painful months that followed, God did a thorough housecleaning of all our hearts, and the change was miraculous.

My parents reconciled, and they were bound together in a way that I never had seen. Not only was the infidelity forgiven, but also years of pain and emotional garbage were swept away. They fell in love with one another as never before. Most importantly, both of them rededicated their lives to our Lord Jesus Christ.

After the craziness of this family-wide conversion had settled into a normal, contented happiness, it was time for me to go off to college. I chose to go to a small, conservative Christian school about an hour north of where I lived. It was perfect. I would live on a beautiful campus and go to school with like-minded individuals who would test and strengthen me in my faith.

It was there that I fell in love with theology—especially the theology of John Calvin. Calvinism made sense. It was clear-cut and (from what I could tell) impeccably biblical. My classmates and I loved to get into debates about the relationship between God's providence and human freedom. I would come down on the side of complete predestination. Anything else, I thought, was an affront to God's sovereignty.

The Fullness of Faith

I spent two happy years inside this very comfortable "college bubble." Then, during the first semester of my junior year, I became friends with a wonderful girl who had the gross misfortune of being Catholic. And unlike the other Catholics that I knew, her faith in Christ was alive and active. Her dad was a former Presbyterian pastor who had converted to Catholicism and founded a Catholic family ministry.

This all was *extremely* odd to me. So I did the only thing a good Christian could do: I tried to save her from the evil clutches of Rome.

We began having long conversations in which we studied the Bible and examined the differences of our beliefs. It was remarkable. When this girl explained the teachings of the Catholic Church, she would use Scripture and reasonable arguments to support her claims. She was very persuasive, and I eventually decided that I needed to take a step back and explore these things for myself. So for the next three months, I went into retreat and immersed myself in prayer and study.

One of the most vivid memories I have of that time occurred while I was reading the letters of Saint Ignatius of Antioch:

> Take note of those who hold heterodox opinions on the grace of Jesus Christ which has come to us, and see how contrary their opinions are to the mind of God.... They abstain from the Eucharist and from prayer because they do not confess that the Eucharist is the flesh of our Savior Jesus Christ, flesh which suffered for our sins and which that Father, in his goodness, raised up again. They who deny the gift of God are perishing in their disputes.[1]

When I read these words, I felt as though I had been hit by a rock. Here was a man ordained by the apostles themselves—a bishop of the ancient church of Antioch, a Christian martyred in the Roman Coliseum—and he was spouting off what I had always considered to be whacked-out, medieval, Roman Catholic, superstitious inventions!

What I had hoped would be a one-time event—finding Catholic theology in the writings of the early Church—ended up occurring over and over again. Purgatory, the sacrifice of the Mass, Mary, the unity of the Church, the papacy: it was all there in the faith of the early Fathers.

As I listened to debates between Catholic and Protestant theologians, I began to find the Protestant explanations unsatisfying. The biblical, historical and theological evidence was building. Half of me couldn't get enough—discovery after discovery made the words of Scripture come alive. My soul had awoken to the beauty and splendor of the unchanging truth of the Catholic Church.

But the other half of me was scared. What would it do to my family if I converted? Would I shatter the beautiful unity we had worked so hard to attain?

The final piece fell into place while I was listening to a tape on the sacrament of matrimony. The Catholic Church has been proclaiming and defending for two thousand years exactly what Christ taught about the indissolubility of marriage and the evils of contraception and divorce. The Catholic Church has stood strong and proclaimed the fullness of the gospel in the midst of cultural changes. After months of reading, praying and listening, I knew that I had to follow Christ into his Church.

I spent the summer of 2003 in private instruction with a faithful priest in my home diocese. On August 3, 2003, I had my first sacramental confession and was received into the Catholic Church. I chose Saint Ignatius of Antioch as my confirmation saint, as it was his journey to the Coliseum and his commitment to the real presence of Christ in the Eucharist that pointed me to the one true Church. And when I finally received what he referred to as "the medicine of immortality,"[2] I could only respond with humble gratitude for a grace most undeserved.

NINETEEN

It Is Well With My Soul

David Alcorn

How exactly *does* a Baptist turn into a Catholic? That is one question I have had to answer many times.

The issue of faith was almost nonexistent in my family. We only attended church on Christmas Eve. So it must have come as quite a shock to family and friends when, at age fifteen, I announced that I wanted to be baptized and become a Christian.

Because it was the only religious experience I had ever known, I sought out my spiritual calling in a Baptist church. I was baptized by full immersion on December 23, 2001, during the Sunday morning service. As I settled into Christian life, I also began to feel a call to ministry.

However, my excitement about Christianity faded rapidly. It seemed that all we did was gather on Sunday morning to sing and hear a forty-five-minute sermon. There is nothing intrinsically wrong with this, of course, but I wanted *more*.

My dissatisfaction with my faith coincided with a new-found interest in religion in general. I studied Judaism and

Islam, but mostly I wanted to know more about Christianity. I particularly wanted to learn why there were so many different denominations.

In April of 2003 I had my first "Catholic experience" in a bookshop in Halifax, Nova Scotia. I had wandered in to investigate what I had read about Catholic Bibles containing more books than Protestant Bibles. I struck up a conversation with the clerk, who encouraged me to pursue my interest in religion and to learn more about the Catholic Church in particular.

Over the summer I began visiting churches from most of the Protestant denominations in my city: Anglican, Baptist, Pentecostal, Presbyterian, United Church of Canada and so on. One day I worked up enough nerve to go to a Catholic parish. I understood absolutely nothing about the Mass, but later I searched the Internet for some kind of guide. What I found transformed my life.

Finding My Way

Ironically, it was through browsing Catholic Web sites that I became familiar with Protestant terms like *sola scriptura* ("by the Bible alone") and *sola fide* ("by faith alone"). I knew that as a Baptist, I believed in the Bible as the sole authority and that I was saved by faith alone, but I had never heard of these "technical" terms. Now I realized that Protestantism rested upon these two pillars of *sola scriptura* and *sola fide*.

I also encountered on the Internet stories of Catholics who were former Protestants. These whetted my appetite for the Catholic faith and led me to a deeper study of what Catholicism is. In order to be fair to both sides, I read anti-Catholic books as well as Catholic ones. However, Karl Keating's *Catholicism and Fundamentalism* blew away all the ridiculous anti-Catholic arguments I had read. He showed *biblically* how the Catholic Church contains the fullness of the gospel.

In my case the first pillar to fall was *sola scriptura*, and Matthew 16:18–19 was the axe that brought it down. "Simon Peter replied, 'You are the Christ, the Son of the living God.' And Jesus answered him, 'Blessed are you, Simon Bar-Jona! For flesh and blood has not revealed this to you, but my Father who is in heaven. And I tell you, you are Peter, and on this rock I will build my Church, and the gates of Hades shall not prevail against it.'"

I heard many explanations that tried to avoid the fact that Saint Peter was the papal "rock," but none of them were satisfying in light of what I saw to be an obvious statement of our Lord. I had no choice but to accept the Catholic interpretation of the passage. I did not know it at the time, but I was already becoming Catholic.

The big issue for me was the presence of Jesus Christ in the Eucharist. I came to realize that no amount of intellectual argument and debate could convince me one way or the other; I had to believe the words of Jesus himself in John 6.

One day it hit me that if Christians can believe that Jesus Christ was born of a virgin, came back from the dead, ascended into heaven and is God Incarnate, then why should there be any problem believing in the real presence of Jesus in the Eucharist? The Incarnation, the Resurrection and the Ascension are—historically speaking—*past events*. The real presence is troubling because it exists in the here and now.

The words of Jesus in John 6:67, after many of his disciples leave him because they can't accept this teaching, are extremely powerful: "Will you also go away?" Our Lord is willing to risk losing some of his followers over the gift of the Eucharist. I had to say, "Yes, Lord, I believe." And from that point on, I have never doubted his true presence in the Eucharist.

Another troubling issue for me was the Catholic view of salvation. I wanted to believe that we were saved by faith alone, not because it was the most biblical idea but because I didn't want to have to "work out [my] salvation with fear and trembling" (Philippians 2:12). I was well aware of James 2:24—"You see that a man is justified by works and not by faith alone"—but giving up my belief in *sola fide* and eternal security was not easy.

I eventually realized that my belief in these things did not necessarily make them true. The actual truth about salvation is dependent upon the love of God, not my doctrinal preferences. And the many passages dealing with salvation make it clear that one has to have faith *and* works in order to follow God. As I look back, I wonder why it took me so long to see it as I do now.

All Is Well

By early 2005 I had made my decision: I wanted to become Catholic. I had been attending Sunday Mass for about a year when I entered the RCIA program in the autumn of 2005. I was received into the Catholic Church at the Easter Vigil of 2006.

I am currently in college, studying philosophy and contemplating a possible vocation to the priesthood. Even as a Baptist I had felt the call to ministry, and this is something that has only grown stronger. I am anxious to see what God has in store for me.

Music is a wonderful thing, especially hymns. As a Baptist I grew quite fond of one in particular, and now I can say with all sincerity that the words of "It Is Well With My Soul" have reached their fulfillment:

> When peace, like a river, attendeth my way,
> When sorrows like sea billows roll;
> Whatever my lot, Thou has taught me to say,
> It is well, it is well, with my soul.[1]

TWENTY

Freedom in Christ

Andy Swafford

When I was in high school, I lived for the moment. Tomorrow would take care of itself, and my only concern was having fun today.

The things that consumed my life were part and parcel the things that constitute the summer dreams of many adolescents across this country: football, girls and especially image. I was a starting linebacker on the varsity squad, and I led the team in tackles during both my junior and senior years. I was a co-captain as well as the team's MVP. To top it all off, I was dating one of the prettiest girls at our high school. I had everything I thought I could want.

After graduation I accepted an offer from a small school in northeast Kansas called Benedictine College. Once again I was living my dream: playing football and upholding an image that exuded confidence.

Internally, however, I was empty. I was never satisfied: never strong enough or fast enough. I spent all my time in the weight room, and I would wake up extra early every morning to ensure my daily run. All I did was train. Athletics became my life, my obsession.

New Perspectives

I was placed in an unusual situation during my second semester. As part of the general curriculum at Benedictine, I was forced to enroll in two theology classes. Although I was initially a bit skeptical, I became enamored with what I learned from the lectures. I had never encountered anything like this before. I learned more in those classes than I had learned in my previous twelve years of Catholic schooling.

I was hooked, and I officially declared a theology major at the end of that year. Unfortunately, this decision was due more to intellectual intrigue than to a conversion of my heart. I didn't plan to make any big changes in my life. Theology was just an interesting topic.

In May our football team went to Paris, France, for an exhibition game. This "vacation" was great at first, but about halfway through the exhibition game I sustained a leg injury and was rushed to the hospital, where I was diagnosed with a broken fibula. The pain was excruciating.

Even worse than the physical agony, however, was the realization that I would be unable to play football that fall. The thing that made me tick—the thing that made me who I was—had been taken from me. I wallowed in depression all summer.

Every now and then I reflected upon the challenging ideas I had studied in my theology classes. Shortly after returning to school, I set up a meeting with my theology professor. I was determined to get to the bottom of some of the issues that I had been thinking about: contraception, premarital sex, the existence of hell and Mary's perpetual virginity, just to name a few.

I fired question after question at my professor, covering a broad spectrum of issues related to faith and morals in just a few hours. He understood my objections, appreciated my perspective and yet gave logical answers as to why the teachings of the Catholic Church were correct. I was amazed. He told me about the Christian morality class that he was teaching that semester and invited me to sign up. "It might be right up your alley."

Already assigned a full schedule of classes, I was hesitant. But the more I thought about it, the more intrigued I became, and I decided that taking the class might not be a bad idea. After all, what could it hurt?

I walked into the morality class thinking we would spend most of our time on all the things the Catholic Church "condemns." I couldn't have been more wrong. Rather than going through a list of "dos and don'ts," we studied what it means to be truly human. I was captivated by the professor's articulation of various philosophical positions and their influence on our modern culture.

Like many Americans, I had been under the impression that *freedom* simply meant being able to make choices. I thought of the freedom to do *what* I want *whenever* I want. I discovered that this was an extremely limited view of liberty. Choice is an important part of freedom, but at its core *true freedom* is the ability to choose the good. True liberty is not freedom *from* authority but rather freedom *for* excellence, goodness and virtue.

I learned that morality is not restricted to the present. I was forced to reckon with the fact that what we do today will affect who we are tomorrow. And after enough "todays" have passed, our character will be determined and established for the rest of our "tomorrows."

The influence of my professor and his class was tremendous. I began attending a campus Bible study on a regular basis. I came to know some priests and monks who worked at the college. My social life also began to change, as I made some great friends who were passionate about the Catholic faith and let it show through their love and generosity. It was ultimately through their support and friendship that I received the strength I needed to change.

Letting Go

There was still one thing, however, that I refused to hand over to Christ: my relationship with my girlfriend. We had been together since high school, and our relationship was an important part of my life. We were very close, and sadly, we frequently let our sinful passions get the better of us.

I remember coming before God and asking if he wanted me to leave the relationship. But even as I asked, he and I both knew that I wasn't ready or willing to let go of this part of my life. An intense inner struggle ensued. I immersed myself in prayer and the liturgy, seeking the strength to do what I needed to do. But I dreaded doing it more than anything else.

As I was driving home for Christmas break, I finally gave consent to God's will. I knew that this surrender had been brewing internally for several months, and now it was finally here. Not only did I consent to God's will, but I was overcome with an inexplicable peace about my decision. I knew what I had to do, and I had the firm resolve to follow through and do the right thing, for my girlfriend's sake and for mine.

I broke up with her as soon as I arrived home. It was extremely difficult for me to leave the relationship—I truly cared for her—but I knew that this was best for us. Most of my high school friends were shocked by the decision. I was different, and many of them didn't quite know how to process the "new Andy" who was standing before them.

To be honest, there were times when I didn't know how to process the "new me" either. I spent most of my time in prayer and study. I read all four Gospels for the first time during that Christmas break. I seldom left the house. It was odd: I had never felt so alone yet so at peace in my entire life. The Holy Spirit poured a fervor into me that burned deep within my bones. Finally, for the first time in my life, I had found something that was truly worth living for— indeed, something even worth *dying* for.

I had finally found the Truth. His name was Jesus, and he had set me free.

By the spring of my sophomore year, I was talking about chastity and virtue to anyone who would listen. The truth that I was studying was so powerful and so rich that I couldn't help but share it with those around me.

God was good to me. Unworthy as I was, he continued to shower his blessings upon me. Shortly thereafter I met an incredible young woman named Sarah. We eventually began dating, and we were married after our graduation from Benedictine. We now have two children.

God takes care of those who are his own. Far from being an arbitrary dictator, he is nothing less than the most loving and committed Father. I am still astounded by how amazing he truly is, and I am forever grateful for the freedom I have found in his one, holy, Catholic and apostolic Church.

TWENTY-ONE

The Battle for Purity

Mike

I was only eleven when I saw my first porno magazine. It was a summer day, and my friend Sam and I were playing in a park located next to a patch of woods. There, under some boards, Sam's older brother had stashed several "adult" magazines. I will never forget the feelings I had at the sight of the naked female body. They were instant and involuntary. At that point Sam and I—a couple of innocent kids who loved playing sports—became victims of pornography.

Later that year another friend showed me his pornography collection, which he kept hidden underneath his dresser drawer. To be honest, I was grossed out at its graphic desecration of the human body and person. I immediately shoved the images away. My friend, finding my response amusing, kept holding them in front of my face, gaily forcing me to look.

This was bad, but things continued to get worse.

In seventh grade I saw my first porn video. A group of us had been playing sports together after school at one guy's house. He led us up to his parents' room afterward and pulled a video out from under their mattress. Gleefully he popped it into the VCR, and we all stood there—looking at each other in embarrassment—as the desecration of God's holy gift of sexuality played before our eyes.

My dad had always instructed me to avoid inappropriate sites when I was on the Internet, so needless to say, I was extremely nervous the first time I looked at Internet pornography. I knew what I was doing: I was making a conscious and deliberate decision to gaze upon impure images. I was young, curious and willing to risk being caught.

I felt anxious when I first typed the search words: "women in underwear." I chose this phrase because I thought it would be less incriminating if I were caught. A link came up, and I clicked it. Immediately I was taken to a disclaimer page stating that all visitors must be twenty-one or over to enter. Only fourteen at the time, I lied—there are many other sins attached to lust—and entered the graphic world of cyberporn.

I can't describe the intensity of my emotions as I entered the site. The only analogy I can come up with is how I feel when I go on a roller coaster: scared, nervous, anxious, doubtful and yet excited. Pictures began to pop up before my eyes. Through my little monitor a whole new world opened up—a world full of sex, nudity, vanity, vice and spiritual death.

I went into the bathroom, and it was there that my world crashed down upon me. This was my first time committing the sin of masturbation. Tragically, it happened at home—only two rooms away from where the rest of my family was peacefully watching TV.

Like most people, I felt enormous shame afterward. My conscience told me how sinful my actions were, and yet, like many boys my age, I allowed myself to be enslaved by what I saw. I was addicted, and slowly but surely the voice of my conscience grew fainter and fainter.

I began looking at Internet pornography for large periods of time every day—about three hours per night on average. This addiction lasted for four years. That means that I spent an average of twenty-one hours a week looking at porn. That's one full day per week that I could have used for playing, studying or spending quality time with family and friends. And to this day I cannot escape the thousands of images that have been sources of lust and moral destruction.

Persisting in Greed

I was fortunate enough to attend a Christian retreat during my senior year. God blessed me during that weekend: My eyes and heart were opened to the saving love and power of Jesus Christ, and I came home excited to be a Christian. I became heavily involved in Bible studies and other Church-related activities.

Things were going well. I was deeply in love with Jesus, and for about a month I resisted pornographic temptation. Until one night, at a friend's Bible study.

The topic for that night's study was simple: sin and forgiveness. During our study the leader told us something that threw me into a moral tailspin. "A sin is a sin is a sin," he said firmly. "In God's eyes it doesn't matter what you do. To him murdering is the same as lying. For Bible-believing Christians, all that matters is that you have Jesus Christ in your heart."

I couldn't believe what I was hearing! He was basically saying—or at least I was hearing—that because I had accepted Jesus as my personal Lord and Savior, I could do whatever I wanted.

It wasn't long before I was right back to my old habits. But this time I was much bolder and more daring. I didn't hesitate to go into my parents' bedroom and get their porno videos out from under their mattress (a favorite hiding place for parents who think they're as sneaky as their children). There was nothing I wanted more than to be free from the filth of my own lust, but I remained captive to my passions.

It wasn't until later in college—when I had started to explore my Catholic roots—that I began to realize just how harmful my sin was. Not only was my impurity an offense to my own dignity and value, but it was also an affront to the dignity of women in general.

I began to go to confession frequently. Let me emphasize that word *frequently*. I desperately needed abundant grace to overcome my addictions to pornography and masturbation. It was a long and painful process.

I still need to be constantly on guard against temptations in this area. Christ's own way of the cross shows us what persistence, submission and hope look like. By the power of his example and grace, I now have the power to pick up my own cross and walk daily with him.

Recommended Resources

Akin, James. *The Salvation Controversy.* San Diego, Calif.: Catholic Answers, 2001.

Aquilina, Mike. *The Fathers of the Church: An Introduction to the First Christian Teachers.* Huntington, Ind.: Our Sunday Visitor, 2006.

Butler, Scott, Norman Dahlgren and David Hess. *Jesus, Peter, and the Keys: A Scriptural Handbook on the Papacy.* Santa Barbara, Calif.: Queenship, 1997.

Cavins, Jeff. *My Life on the Rock: A Rebel Returns to the Catholic Faith,* 2nd ed. West Chester, Pa.: Ascension, 2002.

Courage, a Catholic support group for people dealing with same-sex attractions, www.couragerc.net.

Currie, David B. *Born Fundamentalist, Born Again Catholic.* San Francisco, Calif.: Ignatius, 1996.

———. *Rapture: The End-Times Error that Leaves the Bible Behind.* Manchester, N.H.: Sophia, 2003.

Hahn, Scott. *Catholic Adult Education on Video,* with study guides by Scott and Kimberly Hahn. West Covina, Calif.: St. Joseph, 1994.

————. *A Father Who Keeps His Promises: God's Covenant Love in Scripture.* Cincinnati: Servant, 1998.

————. *Hail, Holy Queen: The Mother of God in the Word of God.* New York: Doubleday, 2001.

————. *The Lamb's Supper: The Mass as Heaven on Earth.* New York: Doubleday, 1999.

————. *Lord, Have Mercy: The Healing Power of Confession.* New York: Doubleday, 2003.

Hahn, Scott and Kimberly, *Rome Sweet Home: Our Journey to Catholicism.* San Francisco: Ignatius, 1993.

Hahn, Scott and Leon J. Surprenant, *Catholic for a Reason: Scripture and the Mystery of the Family of God.* Steubenville, Ohio: Emmaus Road, 1998.

Hart, Mark. *Blessed Are the Bored in Spirit: A Young Catholic's Search for Meaning.* Cincinnati: Servant, 2006.

Healy, Mary. *Men And Women Are From Eden: A Study Guide to John Paul II's Theology of the Body.* Cincinnati: Servant, 2005.

Howard, Thomas. *Evangelical Is Not Enough: Worship of God in Liturgy and Sacrament.* San Francisco: Ignatius, 1988.

Pope John Paul II. *Man and Woman He Created Them: A Theology of the Body.* Boston: Pauline, 2006.

Keating, Karl. *Catholicism and Fundamentalism: The Attack on "Romanism" by "Bible Christians."* San Francisco: Ignatius, 1988.

Kresta, Al. *Why Are Catholics So Concerned About Sin? More Answers to Puzzling Questions About the Catholic Church.* Cincinnati: Servant, 2005.

———. *Why Do Catholics Genuflect? And Answers to Other Puzzling Questions About the Catholic Church.* Cincinnati: Servant, 1996.

Madrid, Patrick. *A Pocket Guide to Apologetics.* Huntington, Ind.: Our Sunday Visitor, 2006.

———. *Pope Fiction: Answers to 30 Myths and Misconceptions about the Papacy.* Irving, Tex.: Basilica, 1998.

———. *Surprised by Truth: 11 Converts Give the Biblical and Historical Reasons for Becoming Catholic.* Irving, Tex.: Basilica, 1994.

———. *Surprised by Truth 2: 15 Men and Women Give the Biblical and Historical Reasons for Becoming Catholic.* Manchester, N.H.: Sophia Institute Press, 2000.

———. *Surprised by Truth 3: 10 More Converts Explain the Biblical and Historical Reasons for Becoming Catholic.* Manchester, N.H.: Sophia Institute Press, 2002.

———. *Where Is* That *in the Bible?* Huntington, Ind.: Our Sunday Visitor, 1999.

McDonough, William K. *The Divine Family: The Trinity and Our Life in God.* Cincinnati: Servant, 2005.

Recommended Resources

Miravalle, Mark. *Introduction to Mary: The Heart of Marian Doctrine and Devotion.* Santa Barbara, Calif.: Queenship, 1997.

Mork, Dom Wulstan. *Transformed by Grace: Scripture, Sacraments, and the Sonship of Christ.* Cincinnati: Servant, 2004.

Olson, Carl E. and Sandra Miesel. *The Da Vinci Hoax: Exposing the Errors in* The Da Vinci Code. San Francisco: Ignatius, 2004.

Pinto, Matthew J. *Did Adam and Eve Have Belly Buttons? And 199 Other Questions from Catholic Teenagers.* West Chester, Pa.: Ascension, 2003.

Ray, Stephen K., *Crossing the Tiber: Evangelical Protestants Discover the Historic Church.* San Francisco: Ignatius, 1997.

———. *Upon This Rock: St. Peter and the Primacy of Rome in Scripture and the Early Church.* San Francisco: Ignatius, 1999.

Schreck, Alan. *Catholic and Christian.* Cincinnati: Servant, 2004.

Scott, David. *The Catholic Passion.* Chicago: Loyola Press, 2005.

Shea, Mark P. *By What Authority? An Evangelical Discovers Catholic Tradition.* Huntington, Ind.: Our Sunday Visitor, 1996.

Trigilio, John and Kenneth Brighenti. *Catholicism for Dummies.* Hoboken, N.J.: Wiley, 2003.

Van Den Aardweg, Gerard J.M. *The Battle for Normality: A Guide for (Self-) Therapy for Homosexuality.* San Francisco: Ignatius, 1997.

West, Christopher. *Good News About Sex and Marriage: Answers to Your Honest Questions About Catholic Teaching.* Cincinnati: Servant, 2004.

Notes

Introduction

1. Saint Augustine, *Confessions,* book 8, chapter 7, n. 17, in John K. Ryan, trans., *The Confessions of St. Augustine* (New York: Doubleday, 1960), p. 194.

2. *Confessions,* book 1, chapter 1, n. 1, in Ryan, p. 43.

3. First Message of His Holiness Benedict XVI at the End of the Eucharistic Concelebration with the Members of the College of Cardinals, Wednesday, April 20, 2005, nn. 3, 6, www.vatican.va.

Chapter Ten: Breaking Free

1. A form of this chapter previously appeared in *Lay Witness Magazine,* January/February 2005.

Chapter Fourteen: Cradle Convert

1. Flannery O'Connor, *Spiritual Writings* (Maryknoll, N.Y.: Orbis, 2003), p. 56.

Chapter Fifteen: Nowhere Else to Go

1. Vatican Council II, Postconciliar Document, "Some General Principles of Particular Importance in Instructing the People of God in the Mystery of the

Eucharist," Chapter I, n. 7, in Austin Flannery, ed., *Vatican Council II: The Conciliar and Postconciliar Documents,* New Revised Edition (Northport, N.Y.: Costello, 1996), p. 107.

Chapter Seventeen: From Belief to Love

1. Jennifer Knapp, "Martyrs and Thieves," www.praisetown.com.

Chapter Eighteen: Indissoluble Love

1. Saint Ignatius of Antioch, Letter to the Smyrnaeans, 6:2—7:1, AD 110, www.Catholic.com.

2. Saint Ignatius of Antioch, Epistle to the Ephesians, chapter 20.2, www.newadvent.org.

Chapter Nineteen: It Is Well With My Soul

1. Horatio G. Spafford, "It Is Well with My Soul," 1873, www.cyberhymnal.org.